CHRIST IN THE TIME OF CORONA

STORIES OF FAITH, HOPE, AND LOVE

GENERAL EDITOR

JOSHUA BURDETTE

Published by White Blackbird Books, an imprint of Storied Publishing

Copyright ©2020 by Joshua Burdette

Permission requests and other questions may be directed to the Contact page at www.storied.pub.

Unless otherwise indicated, Scripture quotations are from the ESV Bible (The Holy Bible, English Standard Version), copyright 2001 by Crossway, a publishing ministry of Good News Publishers. 2011 Text Edition. All rights reserved.

ISBN: 978-1-951991-04-3

Cover design by Jason Bueno

ALSO BY WHITE BLACKBIRD BOOKS

Follow whiteblackbirdbooks.pub for titles and releases.

ABOUT WHITE BLACKBIRD
BOOKS

White blackbirds are extremely rare, but they are real. They are blackbirds that have turned white over the years as their feathers have come in and out over and over again. They are a redemptive picture of something you would never expect to see but that has slowly come into existence over time.

There is plenty of hurt and brokenness in the world. There is the hopelessness that comes in the midst of lost jobs, lost health, lost homes, lost marriages, lost children, lost parents, lost dreams, loss.

But there also are many white blackbirds. There are healed marriages, children who come home, friends who are reconciled. There are hurts healed, children fostered and adopted, communities restored. Some would call these events entirely natural, but really they are unexpected miracles.

The books in this series are not commentaries, nor are they meant to be the final word. Rather, they are a collage of biblical truth applied to current times and places. The authors share their poverty and trust the Lord to use their words to strengthen and encourage his people. Consider these books as entries into the discussion.

May this series help you in your quest to know Christ as he is found in the Gospel through the Scriptures. May you look for and even expect the rare white blackbirds of God's redemption through Christ in your midst. May you be thankful when you look down and see your feathers have turned. May you also rejoice when you see that others have been unexpectedly transformed by Jesus.

CONTENTS

FOREWORD

"It was inevitable: the scent of bitter almonds always reminded him of the fate of unrequited love."[1] This is the opening line in Gabriel García Márquez' landmark novel, *Love in the Time of Cholera*, a story of love, passion, and power in the midst of Colombian civil wars and cholera epidemics of the late 1800s.

I attempted to read it in Spanish in my early twenties while living and teaching in Peru. I tucked my bootlegged copy under my arm and read it in the bars and cafes I encountered while traveling. I even tried to memorize that poignant first line in my awkward Spanish accent. It was a trick I'd hoped to pull off at parties to impress people— and my own fragile ego—into thinking I was a sophisticated man of letters. It never quite worked the way I'd imagined so I eventually abandoned the vain endeavor along with my worn copy of the novel.

Still, the plot and themes of Márquez' novel have come to mind in recent weeks as we have dealt with our own epidemic outbreak and civil angst. In our time, it's not cholera but a coronavirus known as SARS-CoV-2 that marks the season.

In the first months of this year, it became clear that the coronavirus would be a global phenomenon. Epidemiologists warned of high rates of contagion and advised that our best hope to avoid overburdening healthcare systems was to practice widespread social distancing measures.

Life as we knew it changed overnight. States ordered shelter-at-home orders, schools closed, and churches shifted to online worship services. Many employees were told to work from home; others lost their jobs altogether. Still, the death count rose as governors looked for ventilators and hospitals in hot spots looked for space to hold the bodies.

For most of us, however, it wasn't the disease but the prevention that produced painful symptoms. In order to cope, we reached out for virtual connection, we took walks around our neighborhoods, we prayed online together, and we baked lots and lots of bread.

What strikes me now as I reflect on Márquez' novel is the reminder that all human endeavors, whether domestic, vocational, or otherwise, are engaged under the threat and shadow of Death. For those who follow the risen Christ, however, even the most mundane endeavors are also shot through with the beauty and grandeur of another world.

Perhaps that is what we will take away from this crisis: a powerful reminder of human fragility, Divine sovereignty, and the glorious gift of life.

What does it look like for us to be human now, to bear the image of God and our Redeemer in the time of Corona? How do we struggle to be people of faith, hope, and love under a quarantine?

What follows is a collection of essays written while sheltering-at-home during the COVID-19 outbreak as a witness to Christian life in a perilous time. While many of the authors are ordained Presbyterian ministers, this isn't primarily a book about the way you should think or how you should live. Rather, it is a window into our lives. You might say that these stories and observations deal less in what *should be*, and more in what *is*, at least for a small group of like-minded Christians. Hopefully you will also find a glimpse of the world yet to come.

May you find insight and camaraderie among these pages as you seek to follow Christ in the time of Corona.

Rev. Joshua Burdette
Santa Barbara, California
May 1, 2020

---

1. Gabriel García Márquez, Love in the Time of Cholera (Vintage, 1988), 3.

FAITH IN THE TIME OF CORONA

SEPARATING THE BODY FOR THE SAKE OF THE BODY

BRITTANY SMITH

The Absurdity of Absence in the Time of Corona

———

Brittany Smith works as Campus Staff for Reformed University Fellowship at the University of Arizona in Tucson. She grew up in Mesquite, Texas and holds a Masters of Educational Ministry from Covenant Theological Seminary. She is married to Dan, and they have two children. She enjoys the wildlife of the Sonoran Desert, throwing pool parties, and playing Overcooked on the Nintendo Switch with her children. She is the co-editor of Co-Laborers, Co-Heirs: A Family Conversation.

———

Mr. Rogers began his after-school program every day by changing out of his sport coat and loafers, and into his sneakers and zip-up cardigan sweater—a sweater hand-made by his mother.[1] Mothers often notice our body needs before we do. "Take a sweater!" is a trope of the mother whose care has become almost annoying in its accuracy.

When I became a mother, it trained me to pay attention to the body in a mind-shifting way. Babies must be

3

attended to with care. Sometimes your only clue to their thriving or suffering comes by paying attention to their bodies. A flush, a bump, a strange cry that sounded different from the night before. We pay attention to the bodies of our children until we can train them to do it themselves. And though the goal is to hand off this task over to them fully one day, we realize along the way that this body-care was foundational to caring for them as a whole person. Addressing the sufferings and joys of an eight-year-old who can tell you what he is thinking or feeling emotionally still takes attention to the body. Hunger and sleep can contribute to a bad mood just as much as anger or embarrassment. Sometimes we just need a hug.

I work in ministry to college students on a campus. Like any type of Christian ministry or church, one of our main purposes is the care of souls. But our souls are inseparable from our bodies. Quarantine has separated us from our ability to care communally for each other's bodies. Will I notice if my friend is gaining or losing weight? Will I be able to tell if that person in my ministry is experiencing more anxiety? Only if they tell me. I can't rely on the non-verbal clues I used to have to feel confident someone was telling me the truth (or not). I can't pick up on the physical cues that might bely some deeper issue or problem waiting to be unearthed by the tender prodding of a friend.

Curt Thompson, a psychiatrist and Christian writer, helps us understand some of the science behind the fatigue and loss of being physically separated from each other:

> Human beings use our bodies, vis-à-vis our actual words, to communicate upwards to 85–90% of everything we "say." These nonverbal cues—eye contact, tone of voice, facial expression, body language, gestures, timing and intensity of responses—are the body's portion of what it means to "be" with others and ourselves—to

communicate what we are experiencing. We send and we receive vital, live-giving exchanges to each other and this does not require conscious intention to do so. Our bodies are working independently of our conscious, thinking brain, enabling us to love and be loved, to be known and to know, even without the use of words. And this is why we are so much more tired at the end of the day.

Normally, our bodies are able to "say" things when we are in person that we don't have to "think" about otherwise. I can say, "I'm really comfortable with you" or "Wow, I can tell that was really hard" without using words. This enables my "thinking" brain to concentrate on other things. But when I'm on a Zoom call, my "thinking" brain has to make up for what my body is not available to say. Hence, the conscious, cognitive domain of my mind is having to do much, much more work than it is used to doing. And to some degree, like an underdeveloped muscle, it has to work up to speed. But that metaphor only goes so far.

One of several things that COVID-19 has revealed is that our thinking minds are not able to make up for what our bodies—and our bodies alone—were created for. Our bodies, in fact, are looking for the presence of other bodies, as it were—and they're not there.[2]

I had a difficult time with the immediate severing of my regular relationships with students in our college ministry. I saw many of our students more than once a week, which usually included a meal in our home where I sat and watched them eat nourishing food, gave them hugs, laughed with them, and shared more than just presence. I watched their bodies ease away the tension of their school day as they greeted friends. I watched their faces express joy and comfort as they built friendships each week. I'm not their mother, but I found myself watching them the same way I watched my babies when they were young. The words my students say are only part of the story their whole self is telling about who they are, how they are doing, and what care I can give them as a friend. I haven't been able to replicate most of what I called "ministry" via Zoom and phone calls. I'm trying, but I just don't know if there is any way to fully replace bodily presence.

Meanwhile, back on the farm, my normal family unit is my husband and two kids. And when the first stay-at-home orders went into place, I invited my younger brother to relocate temporarily from San Francisco to our casita in Tucson. His office had closed, and he would be working from home alone in his apartment for at least six weeks. He rented a car, loaded what he could into it, including his pug Hobbes, and drove to the Sonoran Desert. Six weeks has turned into ten. He's planning to make his move semi-permanent until his office makes firmer plans for a reopening, which isn't likely until after the summer.

It's been a strange blessing to be bodily separated from all my normal community of people and somehow have this new bodily addition to our family unit. My brother eats all his meals with us, and we've adjusted our meal planning and grocery shopping. He chats with me in person about small daily things we don't usually share with each other in our intermittent phone calls when living a state away from each other. I can tell when he's in a bad mood. He tells me when he had a bad night's sleep or when he stubs his toe in our shower.

I don't usually get to live my life in the bodily presence of my brother for this long. I notice new things about his body: how it's changed with age or the quickness he moves after being stuck at a desk for work most of the day. Our biological family has grown unexpectedly in contrast to the loss of our ministry family.

These are the things I didn't realize I notice all the time about the bodies of people around me—I took so much for granted. Faces and bodies communicate to us more than just through abstract presence; through small movements and subtle changes over time I learn things about a person I could not otherwise know. I miss my friends and my students—I miss their bodies.

I remember in seminary thinking for the first time significantly about Jesus' bodily departure from this earth. He didn't disappear or morph into some other form of spirit. Somewhere out there Jesus reigns and sits with his physical body on the throne. But why did he have to do that? Why did he have to bodily leave us? It seems like a much better idea to stick around and be all together. I used to feel frustrated with how I was supposed to understand Jesus. How could I know he loved me if I couldn't get a hug from him or see his smiling face? Words on a page—even the pages of Holy Scripture—I doubted could be meaningful enough.

Of course Jesus anticipated thoughts and doubts like mine and lovingly pre-answered them in the Gospel of John:

> *These things I have spoken to you while I am still with you. But the Helper, the Holy Spirit, whom the Father will send in my name, he will teach you all things and bring to your remembrance all that I have said to you. Peace I leave with you; my peace I give to you. Not as the world gives do I give to you. Let not your hearts be troubled, neither let them be afraid.* (John 14:25–27)

So I know we have our answer, even though I do not always feel good about it or even fully comprehend it. Jesus bodily distanced himself from us for our own good —and we were given a better gift instead—his own Spirit living inside of us.

I don't think we were created as humans to regularly live socially distanced lives and to bodily separate ourselves from each other. I feel the loss and grief of it as much as anyone. We experience enough bodily separation from each other when our bodies die and we move into whatever waiting period is happening before we are resurrected. But Jesus saw fit to plan a season of bodily separation from his bride. And he provides for us well in the meantime.

Do I really long to be with Jesus the way Paul does in Philippians 1:23? If so, it sure has been easy to distract myself up until now with the presence of others. So if this season of bodily separation for the sake of caring for each other's bodies is wearisome and agonizing, we have something to cling to in how Jesus has provided for us already. This absurdity of absence is not without its heavenly provision.

---

1. Christine Jackson, "The Importance of Sweaters and Sneakers in Mister Rogers' Neighborhood," Rewire.org, March 20, 2017, https://www.rewire.org/sweaters-sneakers-rogers-neighborhood/

2. Curt Thompson, "A Body of Work," curtthompsonmd.com, April 15, 2020, https://curtthompsonmd.com/a-body-of-work/.

GOOD GRIEF
EWAN KENNEDY

Lament in the Time of Corona

———

Ewan serves as the Senior Pastor at Church of the Redeemer in Atlanta, Georgia. Born and raised in Scotland, Ewan started out as a mechanical engineer in the design and management side of the construction industry before coming to the United States as an adult. Ewan has a diploma in Religion from Cambridge University, a BA from David Lipscomb University, and an MDiv and a Masters in Counseling from Covenant Theological Seminary. He is married to Heather and has three sons: Calvin, Cooper, and Canon.

———

We do not like lament. We don't want to do it, we find it awkward, we are uncomfortable when other people are lamenting, and we sometimes fear it is spiritually unhealthy and possibly wrong. In all my years of pastoral ministry, I don't think I've ever had a congregant tell me, "Pastor Ewan, we need to be lamenting more."

The Costly Loss of Lament

Pastors have failed to lead people into lament, but the loss of lament in the church is not just a lack of education. It's a sin of omission. We have failed to worship and engage with God in the way he has prescribed in the Scriptures. If we don't lament, we will pay a cost and so will those around us. During the pandemic, I've seen that cost as a pastor and have also paid that cost personally. As we transition from quarantine to living with the coronavirus, I fear those costs will increase if we don't lean into lament.

When we don't lament, we take our pain, frustration, fear, confusion, and anger out on others and ourselves. We see that clearly all around us. People are snapping at each other more as tempers are frayed. The news reports that domestic abuse, alcohol sales, porn consumption, Netflix, and social media use all increased drastically during the quarantine. These are unhealthy and unsatisfying diversions from our pain. They are substitute gods. We take our struggles, pains, and difficulties to these false gods instead of crying out to God himself.

This is a time for us to actively engage in lamentation. Not just because things are hard, but because God himself calls and urges us to do so. God doesn't just give us a *"Gosh, okay, if you have to, go ahead and have a short cry."* We are given many laments in the Bible. There are more psalms of complaint, imprecation, lament, and struggle than any other type of psalm!

It's more than simply just forgetting to lament. We find lament awkward, unspiritual, wrong, and maybe distasteful. We have paid a cost for this neglect and avoidance. But the bottom line is lament is actually worship, a very important and deep kind of worship. In lament God welcomes and embraces our cries and tears. Our Father wants to hear about our pain, anger, and the questions we have about our world, our situation, where he is, and what he is doing.

We need to take our pain to Jesus. We must lean into the laments God has given us for times like these. Start with Psalm 102, Psalm 88, and Psalm 44.

When God Holds Your Eyelids Open

"Godly despair is… a howling prayer that sees no explanation for our pain but reflexively knows something beyond an answer is what we desire. Godly despair cries out for perspective but allows the hollowness of loss to move the heart to seek God."

Dan Allender, *The Cry of the Soul*

If you continue to engage with the (many) laments in the Bible, it becomes more and more obvious that God is a lot more comfortable with our pain, confusion, questions, struggles, and despair than we are. Laments can feel awkward, even when we read them alone. When we read and enter into laments publicly, whether in church or with our small groups, it's a whole other level of awkwardness! It's a struggle to believe that it's okay for us to talk to God like this. But the Hebrew title for the book of Psalms is "The Book of Public Praises," and there are many laments in the Psalter. We are meant to lament together. God wants us to, and we need to lament together.

We avoid this biblical, Christian practice for many of the same reasons it is important, good, necessary, and healthy. Laments require vulnerability which is difficult especially in public. It is a risk, but vulnerability is the key component for relational health, depth, and intimacy. Love cannot flourish without vulnerability and avoiding it will kill intimacy every single time.

Psalm 77 teaches that God will passionately fight for intimacy with you even if it means causing you pain and discomfort. God is willing to *"hold my eyelids open"* in ways that cause pain (Ps 77:4). Why? Why would God force this when we just want to close our eyes and make it go away? God wants a costly intimacy with us. We have to see and face the pain, suffering, injustice, and loneliness in our own lives and in the world around us. He wants us to experience pain. He wants us to face reality. Why? Because he wants us to come to him vulnerable, in need, and open. He wants all of us, and he knows that we need all of him.

In Psalm 77, like so many other laments, we see that praise and lament go hand in hand. They need each other. When we praise God and remember the good things and the good times, it should, and it MUST, lead us into lament and longing. Why? Because everything is broken, and the good things we experience do not last or soon get spoiled. Things in this world are just not right! God wants to hold our eyelids open so we see the pain, suffering, and struggles of others in a world that is unjust, unfair, and unequal.

Take some time to personally lean into the lament of Psalm 77. As you do, ask God what it is he wants you to see and face. Ask him to give you permission and courage to enter into lament more regularly. Confess and repent for your avoidance of vulnerability and intimacy with him.

Lament As Worship

I preached a short sermon series on lament during the coronavirus. In one of my weekly emails to our congregation, I expressed much of what I have written above. I wasn't prepared for how much I would have to live it during our next worship service and the week after.

During the next Sunday's sermon, I preached about that vulnerability dynamic—its importance and its connection with intimacy and love. And then, after that and off-camera, I personally entered (or was dragged into) lament at a deeper level than I have in a long, long time.

Prior to the service, I had asked our youth pastor to lead our post-sermon Liturgy of Lament. I thought it would be good to have another pastoral face up front. But I wasn't prepared for how this would enable me to participate personally.

As we went through the lament liturgy, in the weird and mysterious work of the Spirit, I knew I was lamenting with my church family—and the tears just came. And then, of course, we went even deeper into lament in song and in prayer. I barely pulled myself together and struggled through the benediction. And then, back in my office, every time I wet to click on the link to enter our post-church drop-in Zoom gathering, anticipating seeing the faces of my church family, I could not hold back the tears.

I just couldn't do it. "Sobbing mess" would have been a fair description. So, I let our other pastors know, and, knowing the flock was in very good pastoral hands, I spent some time alone.

Later that afternoon I heard from others that something important had happened during that Zoom call. The Holy Spirit worked in people connected by technology. People entered into lament, shared vulnerably, and wept together. I was thankful, and yet I was torn.

I questioned my choices: *Did I abandon the flock? Chicken out? Avoid the very vulnerability I had just preached about?* These seemed like all fair (and appropriate) questions. I included a brief apology to the congregation in my Sunday evening email. And then, each day the following week, I heard from so many people about how powerfully God worked through all that mess, all the tears during and after Sunday's worship, and in the laments and vulnerability during the post-church Zoom drop-in, later that week at home, and in our small groups.

My being a non-Zoom-meeting sobbing mess ended up as something that gave permission for others to enter deeper into lament! God works in wonderful and unexpected ways, exactly like Psalm 77 declares! I am so thankful to God for his work and deeply appreciative of all the vulnerability that was entered into and shared. The emails, texts, and phone calls that followed touched me deeply and drew me closer to God. Lament is worship. It really is.

We know lament is worship because Jesus did it. In Luke 19:41–44 we are told:

And when he drew near and saw the city, he wept over it, saying, "Would that you, even you, had known on this day the things that make for peace! But now they are hidden from your eyes."

The word "wept" used here is not the word for quiet, polite crying. It's the word for loud sobbing and wailing. If Jesus sobbed and audibly wailed in lament, we can and should also.

Revelation 6:9–10 tells us the martyrs in heaven lament before God at this very moment. In heaven! In the place where there is no sin or wrongdoing. The saints around the throne are lamenting and questioning God:

When he opened the fifth seal, I saw under the altar the souls of those who had been slain for the word of God and for the witness they had borne. They cried out with a loud voice, "O Sovereign Lord, holy and true, how long before you will judge and avenge our blood on those who dwell on the earth?"

When we avoid lament or feel like it's not right, we are actually saying that we are better Christians than Jesus and the martyrs. We need to let that sink in and bear the fruit of repentance. Lament isn't just something God allows or puts up with. Lament is deep worship that profoundly honors God. For when we lament, we take all our hearts, our desperation, our helplessness, and the rawness of our longings and fears to God as the only one who can help, rescue, comfort, and sustain us.

May you lean into lament during the time of Corona. May Christ lead his church into lament, and by doing so may we truly and deeply meet Christ now and in the days to come.

EYE CONTACT
ROBBIE SCHMIDTBERGER

Preaching to a Camera in the Time of Corona

———

Robbie serves as the Church Planting Pastor of Iron Works Church in West Chester, Pennsylvania. He has a BA in Christian Thought from Grove City College and an MDiv from the Reformed Presbyterian Theological Seminary. He is married to Jennifer, and they have two sons.

———

I remember the week of March 8th really well. West Chester University is just three blocks from my church. With an enrollment of 17,000 students, the university suspended their residential programs while students were on Spring Break. The next day I met with pastors from two other non-denominational churches. One is currently in the midst of a building renovation, so they rent space from the local school district to worship. They became immediately displaced.

My church plant is two-and-a-half years old. We would have been in the exact predicament except when a sister church in our denomination closed, they gave us their two buildings. The luxury of having our own building allowed us to make our own decision. We cancelled worship for the foreseeable future. One hour after our elder board made that decision, my mayor declared a state of emergency in our borough, and the next day our governor declared a state of emergency in our county.

In some ways the decision was made for us. But what did worship look like on Sunday, March 15? And what has worship looked like in the time of Corona?

We've live-streamed a worship service. This decision is ironic, as in the past, I smugly derided live-streaming. In part, this is my confession.

Almost every church in the United States is currently doing this. Some churches meet via a Zoom meeting. Other pastors preach their sermon on Friday, recording it to air on Sunday. Preachers may be in their living room along with their children, or their basement, or at the church. Americans, suddenly, have a partial shared experience with how persecuted Christians have met to worship for the past decade.

As a church plant, and as a Presbyterian congregation, we opted to do a joint live-stream to share resources and not burden our people. The technological ability to live-stream was not available to Christians in the past as they faced plagues and disease. This is new to me, to many in my Reformed Tradition, and to my parishioners.

What is it like in preaching to a camera? It's awkward. It's different. Yet it's the same.

Preaching to a Camera Is Awkward

My wife caught this as I led the liturgy on the first Sunday of Coronatide.

"You looked nervous," she told me as I returned home from worship.

I responded, "You know how you get nervous when you have direct eye contact with someone, and they don't stop looking in your eyes? That is how I felt, but no one was looking back at me."

The room is almost empty, other than the nine others who are there with me. Where should I look? If I look at the volunteers but not the camera, then I remind the viewers at home that they aren't here. Preachers often tell personal stories and jokes. But when your congregation is not there to encourage the preacher by saying "Amen," offering their laughter, even if it is a pity laugh—what do you do?

Every Sunday reminds you of this awkwardness and isolation, but you have to overcome both in order to serve your people.

Either behind or beside the camera is our confidence monitor. It's a TV showing the live-stream. I see the song lyrics, the liturgy, the scripture text, the musicians, and myself. One Sunday morning I wore a khaki blazer. But somehow the lighting made it look like the color gray, so I blended into the gray walls behind me. So I went into my church office where I had a spare cardigan sitting on my chair and put that on instead. But I noticed myself on the TV. My cardigan looked stretched and did not fit well. This confidence monitor became a vanity mirror exposing my flaws.

As the live-stream developed over the past several weeks, we continued to make changes to make it better. One improvement was having floor microphones intended to capture the responsiveness aspect of our liturgy. During practice, I was having a conversation with a deacon from our sister church, praising the work of our own mercy team during the past month, then suddenly the sound technician came over and informed us that he could hear our conversation through the audio system. I begin to think through the conversation I just had. Did I share anything private? Was it an inappropriate conversation? (No. And it wasn't.) But I felt exposed once again. I could tell you the time I tripped over a camera tripod, bumped into a chair, or when I put my coffee thermos in the wrong place and the preacher kicked it over just as he began to preach.

Preaching to a Camera Is Different

Preachers are accustomed and taught to preach to a room full of people. While many churches have live-streamed their worship for several years now, a live-streaming in the time of Corona is different. The room is empty. Your church is scattered.

We see the church scattered before. Consider the early church: *On that day a great persecution broke out against the church in Jerusalem, and all except the apostles were scattered throughout Judea and Samaria... Those who had been scattered preached the word wherever they went.* (Acts 8:1,4)

God uses trials not only to reveal our character and maturity, but also to propel us forward and to grow. The apostles remained in Jerusalem, until persecution came. Persecution drove the apostles to obey Jesus' great commission to go to the ends of the earth.

While I'm a pastor called and bound to a local church, suddenly I am a preacher without an audience. The Reformed tradition emphasizes gathered worship as its where one sees the ordinary means of grace via prayer, word, and sacrament. The shift that pastors find themselves in is that we are not preaching to a gathered church but the church scattered.

A preacher's focus must be different. In gathered worship, we put a lot of effort and preparation into congregational worship, then small groups, and then family ministry. But during the time of Corona, preachers serve their congregations by being their pastor. If preachers put the same effort into pastoral care that they normally put into preaching, then the church will grow and thrive.

Preaching to a camera is clearly different. This is how we see God being redemptive in this moment. But just because good things come out of crisis does not mean it is a good thing. The church is scattered, and this is not a good thing.

Hebrews tells us:

> And since we have a great priest over the house of God, let us draw near with a true heart in full assurance of faith, with our hearts sprinkled clean from an evil conscience and our bodies washed with pure water. Let us hold fast the confession of our hope without wavering, for he who promised is faithful.
>
> And let us consider how to stir up one another to love and good works, not neglecting to meet together, as is the habit of some, but encouraging one another, and all the more as you see the Day drawing near. (Heb. 10:21–25)

Look at the argument the author of Hebrews makes. Christians have a great high priest in the person of Jesus Christ. Because of what Jesus did for us in his life, death, and resurrection, we are able to come before God. Christians, however, are the house of God. This is a beautiful picture abounding in the Old Testament, as the house of God was the temple. The temple signified God's dwelling with his people. So as the house of God, let's come before God without hesitation and enjoy the gift of being forgiven from our sins. We have life with God.

But how do you encourage one another to love and do good works?

You encourage one another to love and do good works by meeting together.

Every Sunday we are reminded of something that we lost. And this is in addition to the lost income, graduations, weddings or romantic getaways, saying goodbye to friends who've moved with a hug, live music at your favorite restaurant, and more. We lack the gift of shaking someone's hand, giving them a hug, seeing tears in people's eyes as they share a hardship or the news that they are expecting. We lack the gift of hearing one another praise the Lord together, hearing spontaneous voices exclaim God's praises, passing the peace to one another, or praying over the children as they are sent to their classes. We've lost the gift of receiving new members by profession and baptism. We've lost the Lord's Supper for a time.

That hurts.

Perhaps you noticed something missing from that list: the preaching of God's word. Preaching to a camera is different because the wonderful body of Christ is absent in hearing it. But preaching to a camera is a gift because it ensures that God's people hear God's word and are stirred to love and good deeds, which are vital in every season but especially in a pandemic.

Preaching to a Camera Is the Same

The prophet Isaiah tells us that God's word does not return empty, *"but it shall accomplish that which I purpose and shall succeed in the thing for which I sent it"* (Is. 55:11). When preachers preach to an empty room and when they lack encouraging amens or laughter to motivate them, what fuels them?

Faith in God to act upon his promises.

I've become more aware of the promises God makes in regard to his Word, and I'm holding on to them tightly and taking them to him in prayer. What are the things for which God gave his word? What does God want to accomplish by his word?

The psalmist declares, *"The heavens declare the glory of God"* (Ps. 19:1). We know about our incredible God from his general revelation in nature. Paul writes in Romans, *"For his invisible attributes, namely, his eternal power and divine nature, have been clearly perceived, ever since the creation of the world, in the things that have been made"* (Ro. 1:20). But this knowledge is limited. God's word is necessary to tell us his story of this world so that we'd have life with him.

God's word is vital for our faith. This is why God gave it to us.

Even though the vanity mirror is there to help us look

good, God's word is not given to make us look good. Preachers must remember this. Our calling is to equip the saints for the work of ministry (Eph. 4:10). Timothy wrote:

> *All of scripture is breathed out by God and profitable for teaching, for reproof, for correction, and for training in righteousness. That the man of God may be complete, equipped for every good work.* (2 Tim. 3:16)

God's word must be listened to, as the parable of the sower shows us that the Christian life is a listening life. When we have a heart that is ready to hear God's word and our ears listen to him, then we will grow and become more like Jesus. Here is how he put it himself:

> *As for what was sown on good soil, this is the one who hears the word and understands it. He indeed bears fruit and yields, in one case a hundredfold, in another sixty, and in another thirty.* (Matt. 13:23)

The incredible truth is that God acts through his word. While we create things out of hammer and nail, God simply spoke this creation into existence (Ps. 33:6). He even upholds the universe by the word of his power (Heb. 1:3). Jesus is Lord over creation, that even when he told the storm to stop raging and be still—it listened (Mark 4:39). God makes us his children through his word. We are born again, regenerated, by the power of God's word (1 Pet. 1:23). When God's word abides within you, then the truth sets you free (1 John 2:14; John 8:32). God exposes our sin by the power of his word:

> *In the beginning was the Word... In him was life, and the life was the light of men. The light shines in the darkness, and the darkness has not overcome it.* (John 1:1, 4-5)

God's word convicts us of our sin, comforts us when

we are hurting, and confirms his love for us. When I preach to a camera, do I have faith in God to deliver on his promises? He says he will regenerate people's hearts so that I'll see conversions. He says that his Spirit will bring about conviction, revealing his holiness while also revealing his word to us. We are sanctified by truth as God's word is truth (John 17:17).

As a preacher, I must remember all these things and hold on to them in faith. Preaching was never about making me look good. Preaching is about making God famous. He must increase. I must decrease.

The call of preaching is always the same: *"The grass withers, and the flowers fall, but the word of our God will stand forever"* (Is. 40:8).

TESTING POSITIVE
LAURA ANDERSON

Corona in the Time of Corona

———

Laura is a therapist at Midtown Nashville Counseling center. She has a degree in Psychology from Davidson College and a Masters in Counseling from Covenant Theological Seminary. She is married to Ryan, and they have three girls.

———

My husband tested positive for COVID-19. This is our story.

Day 00: Contraction. Saturday night, March 7, my husband Ryan and I attended our school auction. Since then, over fifteen of our friends have been confirmed to have COVID-19, and this seems to be the common denominator place where all of us contracted the virus. There were finger foods, passed plates, and shared pens there, but who knows how it all happened.

Day 01: Onset of symptoms. Tuesday morning, March 10, Ryan went to work, and then I met him at school to read to Evangeline's class. He said he was tired, but since we'd had a big weekend, and he'd had an early morning, we didn't think much of it. At 1pm he called and said he was so was so tired he couldn't work. He needed to come home and sleep for an hour, and then he would work from home. His temperature was 99.5 degrees. Much later that evening, he awoke to a 103-degree temperature with aches and chills. This was the moment I suspected he had COVID-19 because just a few weeks earlier he had the flu, and this presented a bit differently to me. He sweated most of that night and didn't sleep well.

Day 02: He awoke in the morning with some chest tightness and a 100-degree fever and decided to call our infectious disease doctor friend to see at what point and where he should get tested for COVID-19. There were only two cases in the state at that point so it felt rare, but not impossible since he's a pastor and often in large groups. Our friend let him know that he was not the first person in our community to call him that morning with those symptoms, and that he knew of a confirmed case with the same symptoms who had been with us Saturday night.

At this point, I was positive it was COVID-19. I canceled the rest of my clients, picked up the girls from school, and self-quarantined immediately. Our friend told Ryan to go to any Vanderbilt Walk-in Clinic to get tested. They came out to his car with a mask, shield, and gloves and swabbed his nose. They said it would take about twenty-four hours to get results, but I know other states took longer. They didn't prescribe anything other than pain reliever. He did have some more chest congestion and a slight cough, but it didn't keep him from sleep. He slept well.

Day 03: He had energy and no fever. We thought, "Wow that wasn't so bad, not mild per se but pretty quick!" Twenty-four hours later, we got the news he had tested positive. The Health Department asked for the temperatures of everyone in the household (this would become a daily call), and they told us no one in the house could leave until fourteen days after he recovers because of viral shedding. Also, recovery is defined as seventy-two hours after his last symptom. Later that evening he had a 100-degree fever and was tired and achey.

Day 04: He had a 99-degree fever but an appetite. We thought he was improving. He didn't sleep well.

Day 05: He slept in and then napped alot in the day. He had a 100-degree fever. He ate a normal lunch. He didn't eat dinner and went to bed at 8pm with a 100.7-degree temperature and was shaking with chills. His chest was congested and sore, but he didn't cough that much, and hasn't said anything about a sore throat or runny nose.

We live with Ryan's dad right now, so we have Ryan quarantined in an upstairs bedroom. He wears a mask whenever we talk to him. I mostly talk to him on the phone. We drop food at his door at meal times. Today I feel like he hit an emotional sadness wall. I think the long-term isolation is worse than the virus, at least for our age group.

We are learning the recovery is not linear and might continue into week two. I would not call it mild but maybe *moderate plus*? It's not as bad as the flu but more unpredictable. The fever, aches, and chest soreness seem to be the worst part. It would be helpful to know what a mild case looks like. We are trying to take it one day at a time, but it is super depressing and overwhelming to think about 17+ more days like this not to mention all the implications of taking that much time off of life.

We have felt upheld by the church—Christ's people—as they have brought groceries, meals, wine, creative activities for the girls, prayers, quarantine humor, and check-ins to help mitigate the isolation. I believe we'll all make it through this, and by all I mean ALL because no one remains unaffected by this virus.

I am miraculously fine. So are the girls and Papaw,

praise God. I have heard that women and kids are less affected by it, but I do have several girlfriends who have it (and I think being a mom with coronavirus is way harder than being a dad with it, just sayin').

I slept in a bed with Ryan on Day 01 and did normal life with him for three days before the results came back. I shared a bathroom and toothpaste with him Day 01 and 02. Maybe I'm COVID-19 positive but asymptomatic? Maybe I should get tested and see because that would be good information to know? Maybe I am a ninja at avoiding all the germs in the house? I'll say one thing—I touch my face all the time! Also, I haven't washed my kids' hands non-stop—it's too hard. But I try to remember before we eat. Maybe it's God's mercy? I feel more overwhelmed by the 17+ day quarantine than the virus, but I do worry about what would happen if I got it, and who would take care of the kids? I guess at that point, we would just surrender and everyone would get it.

UGH. I know this is a time to run to Jesus because he is the one who ultimately reigns over this crowned virus. It has felt too much for our city between the tornados that hit two weeks ago and the virus. I feel sad and shutdown.

I have found myself not wanting to take refuge in Jesus because I was in a fight with him before all this. I sometimes feel like following him makes my life more frustrating and disappointing, which is likely a combination of my attachment style, my story, my sin, my good longings, the brokenness of the world, and spiritual warfare.

I promise all of you, I am not good at following Jesus —just ask my husband when he's better. I think Job's wife and I could have been fast wine-drinking friends! But I have to keep wrestling because I believe the gospel is true cognitively and experientially. So I guess Jesus is not done with me yet. Tonight I carry the weight of my clients' unfinished stories, my own unfinished story, the wake of tornado destruction though our city, and the continued unknowns of COVID-19. My only hope for tonight (and any other night for that matter) is not in my affection for Jesus or how well I trust him when the world's falling apart, but in his unfailing affection and covenantal faithfulness to me.

Also, send wine.

Ryan has since recovered from COVID-19 and is doing well.

FEED MY SHEEP
DAN QUAKKELAAR

Shepherding in the Time of Corona

———

Dan is the pastor at Friend of Sinners Mission Church in inner-city Milwaukee. After serving in the military and a twenty-year career in the magazine publishing industry, Dan left his position as an executive and went to Covenant Theological Seminary. He and Shereen have been married since 1982, and they have raised five children.

———

People love to help the poor or help victims during a time of crisis. People want to accomplish tangible success with their financial help and volunteer efforts.

After SARS-CoV-2 hit, donations began to come at a faster pace than normal for Friend of Sinners Mission Church in inner-city Milwaukee. This outpouring of love was generous, except it was designated only for mercy ministry.

Those without food will get deliveries. Friend of Sinners always fed the poor, but now we do it with additional mercy funds, and our donors enable this generosity.

A sense of thankfulness motivates us as we shepherd during deliveries. We fellowship across the thresholds of homes and pray through masks and gloves and windows and doors.

It is not as if the needs are less. They are different. We have new needs for the vulnerable who should not be at the grocery store because they are at risk. For these, and especially for the infirmed who are still living at home, we are working a lot harder at delivering groceries we would not have delivered previously. My wife Sherry has been cooking freezer meals so that those who have trouble cooking for themselves are able to just pop a meal in a pan to heat up.

It takes a lot of time, but my Sherry loves to cook. We eventually hit a rhythm of taking in requests for food daily, compiling those and evaluating them, and preparing a list for the grocery store that she can chip away at as she travels. We need to work around store-imposed rationing to buy what we need. Sherry puts together a route and a schedule. By Friday or Saturday all the food is in, and we deliver it, or people come to our home to pick up what we set aside.

But feeding the sheep is not just about physical food. The Holy Spirit provides spiritual food and guidance through us and others as we go. We bear one another's burdens. And in the time of Corona, we hunger in new ways and this often requires new solutions for delivering that spiritual nourishment. Zoom meetings, Marco Polo, Next Door, and six-foot conversations during the walks to get my step count higher. I am multitasking for the Lord.

The homeless population changed a bit after SARS-CoV-2. They look more like me: no criminal history, no history of drug use, no history of mental health issues. I have never seen that before.

A week ago, we discovered a single woman, Jaleese, living in the bus station in downtown Milwaukee. No kids. Two bins of belongings. She has a degree from a top school, and she was a teacher's aid working toward her teaching certificate. She had lost her job, and with school closings, she did not find new work. She lived two days in the bus station downtown. There is no room for her in drug rehab places since she is not an addict. They will not take her, even as a volunteer, and the state quarantined many of the shelters because SARS-CoV-2 infections were found. The open shelters will only take her if she has kids. Without help from someone else, she falls through the cracks.

We contacted her by phone one night just as the temperature began dropping below freezing. She was in danger; not just from the cold. Predators commonly scout for single women without protection out on the street. They will take her money and sexually abuse or rape her. Most women on the street without help know they must find a strong man to protect them in exchange for sexual favors. This is the reality, typically. But these new homeless enter this danger zone unaware of all of that.

We worked with another partner church to get Jaleese into a hotel. It expends resources, but her prospects for getting back on track are great. Those extra resources could facilitate a change in her situation. Nothing is sure. I hand it off to the partner church, thankful to pass along this situation given my workload.

Grieve and move on. Grieve and move on.

Preparing for Sunday

Sherry and I rent a place across from a high school. We love our home in the city. Kind people live around our home, people who desire to protect and honor the "Man of God" in our nearly all-Black neighborhood. The culture still requires that the Man of God not be touched. There is faith here beyond what I have experienced in the suburbs. Evangelism on the streets turns up many brothers and sisters who quote long memorized passages from Scripture. I rejoice at the faith poverty brings. Neighbors live day by day, trusting that the Lord will wake them in the morning. This faith walk intensified as SARS-CoV-2 infection spread.

My office is an upstairs bedroom in that house, converted into a little study. In the morning I wander a dozen steps from my bed down the hall to my desk. I use this small study to prepare the spiritual meal for Friend of Sinners Mission Church. We will live-stream Sunday morning.

Sherry goes downstairs to get me coffee. I look at my fitness watch, and registers eleven steps. I feel cheated; I took at least fifteen. I need to get to 6,000, and I cannot seem to get outside to walk. Every step counts.

I hear rustling in the wall. Squirrels nest in the soffits. I tried to catch them. If they die in there, they will stink up the house. They already chewed the wires for the garage door sensor, which I fixed several times now. The landlord gave me a trap, but the squirrel seems too smart for that. The mice in the basement demonstrate the same survival abilities. We tried so many traps, but the mice figured them all out. They run free, without any social distancing at all!

I realize my distraction. I can fight the squirrels and mice later. Preparation for Sunday awaits. I switch the computer on.

My first task is to get the bulletin into shape. I have a template. The songs are picked by the worship team. I look in the Music Team group on Facebook to see if someone posted the songs yet. I plan out liturgical elements for a year, so I need not make any decisions. Plug it in, Dan. Let's go.

As I start Facebook, I start getting distracted by issues that push my buttons but then realize these need to wait. The songs are posted. Good. I get to start my sermon prep which is my favorite part of the week. I love soaking in God's Word. It is a restful place of discovery and inspiration. Simple truths rise majestically from the text. My heart calms. I find grace and safety in the arms of God.

Galatians 3—those foolish Galatians. I sit down and

begin my work in the Greek text. Foolishness is not foolishness, but lack of understanding.

The phone rings, and I try to ignore it. I don't need another car warranty. Sherry answers it.

Foolishness. Right. And this other word, bewitched! That looks interesting. Not witchcraft, but evil influence. Witchcraft light? Hmmm.

I hear Sherry downstairs talking. No, she is coming up the stairs. This is a church call, I know it.

"Dan?"

"Yup."

"Janice."

"Oh. Is she okay?"

"Well, she's at her brother's and they need food."

"Where are the kids?"

"Still with Charles."

I freeze a little inside. Charles has a history of domestic abuse and an outstanding warrant. He and Janice are married with four kids. Charles does not know where her brother lives. She goes there to escape danger.

"He threatened her and hit her, but no bruises, she said. She had to leave the kids behind."

I know Charles has never hurt the kids, but I find no comfort in that. Elenore, the Grandma, already moved out after he turned on her too.

"How much food do we have?" I ask Sherry.

"I can put something together from what we have. I'm making a grocery store run tomorrow."

I know that we received many mercy gifts, but I need to replenish the mercy debit card Sherry will need. It's a good reminder. Oh, and I need to check if webcams came down in price. I need a new one of those to replace the old one. I realize I am distracted again.

Sherry knows. "You need to talk with Charles."

"I'll try and get him on the phone. He does not answer. I might need to go over there."

"Go with leadership then."

She is right. The two most dangerous activities in the

inner city are drug use and domestic abuse. I should not go alone. And I will need my mask. The gentle shepherd comes with a mask on. A real mask. Not the old one that no one saw before SARS-CoV-2, hopefully. Not the mask that hides my frustration. Just the one that prevents me from spreading disease, if I am infected.

"I'll text him and let leadership know."

She looks at me, waiting for me to text Charles. She loves me. She is a true helper.

"She's safe right now. I'm working on my sermon." I think of the kids.

"Well that's important too. You're right."

I text Charles, knowing he will not answer, but at least the ball is in play. I feel tension rising in me. I look at Sherry.

"I just need to be left alone." I'm getting loud. "I want to finish Just. One. Thing." I say in frustration. But I know the job is never finished. I am frustrated. My counselor would ask me to consult my feeling wheel. Counselors provide the ability to see things in a new way. New perspective often produces illumination. But the counselor thinks I struggle to understand my feelings. I hate the feeling wheel. It insults me. But I wonder if she is right. Perhaps in the time of Corona I struggle to hide my emotions more.

I go back to my sermon research.

Galatians 3:4—vain. Do we suffer in vain? That will preach, I think. God leans down and touches my heart. "Is it in vain?" I ask him. I do not want to think about it, but I do, and the tears come.

Sherry is at the door. She looks at me. "I'm concerned about a breakdown."

Great. One more thing to worry about.

"Honey, I don't know how to fix it. I love this calling, this vocation. I love the people of God at Friend of Sinners. I love the neighborhood we live in and the neighborhood of church. I even love the lost. I just want to do one thing at a time."

"I know. How can I help you do that?"

"I don't know. I love you. Thank you for loving me."

Sherry is my joy. Everything she does is gold.

Meanwhile, I feel a lingering vanity in my own efforts.

Vanity of vanities, says the Preacher, vanity of vanities! All is vanity. What does man gain by all the toil at which he toils under the sun? A generation goes, and a generation comes, but the earth remains forever. The sun rises, and the sun goes down, and hastens to the place where it rises. (Eccl. 1:2–5)

Thank you, Solomon. Preacher-man.

I stare at verse four. The Spirit pulls me into meditating on his provision. I see Paul pouring into his argument precious Old Testament quotes in Galatians 3:

"Abraham believed God and it was counted to him as righteousness."
"In you shall all the nations be blessed."
"Cursed be everyone who does not abide by all things written in the Book of the Law, and do them."
"The righteous shall live by faith."

I rest in his Word.

Loss

An hour later I need to find a place to stop. I do not want to stop, but I must. Today is the funeral of Aleisha Scott-Dunn, forty-one years old, mother of three, ages sixteen to twenty-one, husband in jail. She died of complications from asthma. My heart aches again.

Aleisha began attending at Friend of Sinners with her family right away. She discipled me in so many ways. Sherry and I met her at Carver Park. There we were, two white adults in a sea of color, trying to give away brats and potato salad. Like someone would trust white strangers giving away free food for no apparent reason in segregated Milwaukee.

But Sherry dipped her ivory white toes in the wading

35

pool with all the kids, and somehow that broke the barrier. When Aleisha came to eat with us, the rest of the park noticed. People gathered. Who doesn't love free picnic food, and I'm a good griller for brats and burgers.

"Where are you from?" she had asked all those years ago.

"Friend of Sinners Church. We're just starting. I'm Pastor Dan," I said with a smile.

"Oh!"

We sat and chatted for a few minutes.

"When are you bringing the Word?" she suddenly asked.

"Well, we're just here meeting people right now. I didn't plan to preach."

"Aren't you a church?"

I stare back. Yes, we are a church. But this is not the plan, and I have nothing prepared. Except God warned me to be prepared in and out of season to provide a defense of what I believe.

"Aren't you a pastor?" she said, with that look in her eye that I would become so familiar with over the years. She was young, but she was a good, strong mama. She wanted to hear the Word of God. Churches feed people. Not just food—truth.

I preached. And the next week too. Spiritual food.

Aleisha became a precious sister to me and blessed the church richly with her singing and prayer for us and prayer in the fellowship during services. She loved the Lord. She actively discipled her children. She discipled me. Frankly, she pastored me—my Priscilla.

Every year it seemed she would wind up in the hospital in a coma at some point. When it first happened, I was terrified for her and the kids. It became way too routine. The call would come. "Aleisha is in the hospital." And I would go to pray with her, anoint her with oil, and read Scripture.

The last time it happened, two weeks ago, I was

prohibited from seeing her. Coronavirus. But I had called the charge nurse and I thought, "You know, I bet I could sneak in if I wore my collar and brought a Bible." I dressed in my "uniform" and began to head to St. Joseph's Hospital. I was heading out the door when the call came. It was her son, sobbing. She was gone. I was too late.

So here we were once again, two white people in a sea of color in segregated Milwaukee, leading a funeral service where I felt inadequate. With a mask on. I occupied a place of honor that seemed so out of place, and I was grieving myself.

Grieve and move on. Except I can't move on this time. She was my sister. I still miss her.

Chaos

Later Janice texts Sherry. "I lied on Charles. God forgive me for lying and cheating on him. He did too."

What does that mean?

She is back with him, we discover. Back with him.

The next day Elenore calls. "Janice doesn't answer the phone. I haven't been able to talk with her. I think something happened." She begins to cry. "He did something to my daughter."

I call the phone. One of the children answer.

"Can I talk with your Dad?"

"He's not here."

"Can I talk with your Mom?"

"She's sleeping."

I picture Janice laid out on the bed, knocked out and in a coma or something.

I say goodbye and hang up.

I let leadership know there is an issue.

I am insufficient.

I consider using the telephone number I have for Charles, but he does not know I have it. He will know Janice gave it to me, and that might make him angry with her. Do I want to use it? Is this the emergency that makes it necessary?

And why did I hang up on the kids so quickly? That was stupid. I call the kids back.

"Wake her up. I want to talk with her."

I hear groaning. It sounds like her voice. She is disoriented.

"This is Pastor Dan. Are you okay?"

"Yeah, sorry, I was sleeping."

I am relieved and frustrated at the same time. I need my feeling wheel.

"You went back to Charles."

"Yeah."

"Sherry got a text from you. Was that really from you?"

"Yeah."

"So, you lied about the abuse, and you cheated on him?"

"Yeah."

"I have some flowers for you from church for Mother's Day, can I bring them to you right now?"

"Yeah."

I get my mask. Sherry and I leave for her home. Confused. Praying. Sherry stays in the car as I walk up to the door. The kids come.

"Hey Pastor Dan!"

"Hey kids! Is your Mom here? I'd like to give her these flowers from church."

"I can take them."

"But I would like to give them to her myself."

I need to assess her condition. One of the kids goes back inside. They look okay. Janice comes to the door. She smiles. She looks like herself, except her hair is dyed red, and her skin is discolored around her neck.

"Are you okay?"

"Yeah, I'm fine."

It was a dumb question. Of course, she is going to say she is fine.

"That looks like bruising on you neck." I noticed she walked okay. I see no pain, no favoring of a limb.

"Oh yeah, that's from the hair dye." She lifts her hair and shows me stains from the red hair dye.

I give her the flowers and tell her to call me if she has problems. I do not know what is true. Charles can quote Scripture freely. The kids are catechized. They know the doctrines of the church at a young age. They are impressive.

I smile and pray with her. I give her my departing words. She does not look me in the eye. Is it shame or deception? I cannot tell. I go back to the car. We drive home.

Sabbath

I wander back upstairs. I have 1,049 steps on my watch. I do not care.

I accomplished nothing today. It feels that way.

I want to provide extreme generosity to those I shepherd, and to my lost neighbors. I want them to see in this generosity the love of Jesus. I want them to hear the Gospel. I want them to place their trust in Jesus. I want them to know that we all die; we all live in the shadow of death. But Jesus conquered death!

The Spirit comes again. "Don't forget David," he says.

He guides my mind to the cave of Adullam, David's stronghold.

David was then in the stronghold, and the garrison of the Philistines was then at Bethlehem. And David said longingly, "Oh, that someone would give me water to drink from the well of Bethlehem that is by the gate!" Then the three mighty men broke through the camp of the Philistines and drew water out of the well of Bethlehem that was by the gate and carried and brought it to David. But he would not drink of it. He poured it out to the LORD and said, "Far be it from me, O LORD, that I should do this. Shall I drink the blood of the men who went at the risk of

their lives?" Therefore he would not drink it. These things the
three mighty men did. (2 Sam. 23:14–17)

How could David be such a jerk? These men risked their lives to give him a drink of water from his hometown well, and he dumps it out on the ground. I used to think that's what this was about.

But that is not what is happening in this passage.

Only the Lord was worthy of that drink of Bethlehem water. David gives it to the Lord. He says, The work done was done for you. You deserve the reward. It was not wasted. It was worship.

I realize that a day full of masked service is not service for my people, or my wife, or even for me. I am pouring myself out before God. It is to his glory. Nothing is wasted.

I pour myself out.

May God be glorified in the work he produces in his servant. My efforts always fall short. His work never falls short.

GRIEVING LOSS AND REORDERING OUR LOVES

BECKY KIERN

Hitting the Wall in the Time of Corona

———

Becky is a graduate of Covenant Theological Seminary who has served in staff and lay leadership roles in multiple churches. She lives in Nashville, Tennessee, where she teaches the Bible at retreats and conferences, develops church leadership, and writes Bible study curriculum. She is the author of Our Light and Life: Identity in the Claims of Christ *and has contributed to other works including* Co-Laborers, Co-Heirs: A Family Conversation *and* Beneath the Cross of Jesus: Lenten Reflections. *Becky has been an adult cardiology RN for nearly fifteen years. Above all her favorite roles are that of friend, sister, and auntie.*

———

When 2019 ended, I raised my glass and rejoiced at the conclusion of one of the hardest years of my adult life. I was thrilled to enter into 2020, seeing it as a new year filled with new potential. The first half of my year was planned to the max with travel, speaking engagements, conferences, teaching Bible study groups at my local church, and the publication of my first solo writing project. There was excitement, joy, and expectation; after a season of wandering, I felt as if I finally had direction and was gaining traction.

During the first weekend of March, I was on a trip with friends in South Carolina when I got word of the first COVID-19 infection in Nashville, my hometown. As I travelled home on Monday morning, I found myself walking through empty airports and flying home on empty planes—the spring of 2020 had officially begun. Over the course of the next two weeks, my 2020 calendar went from full to numbingly blank, as every event I was attending or leading was (understandably) canceled. I spent hours on the phone with friends, crying about lost events, anxious about firings and furloughs. And I, like so many, had to learn to work from home in a job which was never meant to be done through a flat, cold, computer screen.

On Monday, March 23rd, I finally hit a wall. It became apparent that no amount of wealth, education, or social connection could prevent the experience of loss. This beast was going to deeply affect us all in some way. Any semblance of control seemed to be slipping away, and the collective experience of loss left me feeling as if I were swimming against a rip tide of grief and fear.

One thing I appreciate about the Bible is how it never sugar-coats the consequences of the Fall (Gen. 3:6–8; Rom. 3:23; Eph. 2:1). Read all of its pages and never once will you find it saying, "I know Adam and Eve made a mistake, but it wasn't really that bad." When you read the whole narrative of scripture you find real counsel written by real people who lived in the real world. Its pages are filled with the Lord's faithfulness towards unfaithful, fear-filled, broken men and women, and on that March day (and many other days) I was one of those broken women. I could not make sense of what God was doing, I could not pull myself out of my sorrow, and I could not fix the problems laid before us.

To be clear, I love the Bible not because it honestly

reflects the darkness found in our world, but because on every page it reveals God in his steadfast love and power overcoming that darkness (Matt. 5:17; Jn. 1:5, 16:33; 1 Jn. 1:5). The book of Habakkuk is just one example; its words have been my greatest source of hope and humility in the last eleven weeks. The short but impactful book opens with the prophet Habakkuk voicing his fear to the Lord. He sees injustice, immorality, and pain all around him, and he has had enough—you could say Habakkuk has hit *his* wall.

But even as Habakkuk comes to the end of himself, his expressions of complaint are all addressed directly to Yahweh (Hab. 1:2,12 & 3:2, 18–19). Habakkuk knew with whom he was wrestling, and that made all the difference (Gen. 2:7; Ex. 3:13–15; 2 Sam. 7:23–24; Ps. 6). The prophet brought his fear before Yahweh, the covenant-making, covenant-keeping God, and in his care Habakkuk's fear was transformed into bone-deep faith (Hab. 3:16). The end of the account shows us a man who choses to trust and rejoice, not because the Lord removes all his sorrow, but because the Lord is his Rock, salvation, and strength amidst the sorrow (Hab. 2:12; 3:18–19).

When I hit my wall on March 23rd, I laced up my sneakers, took a long, tear-filled prayer walk, and then sat down and made three lists. The first was a therapeutic unloading of all the losses in this season—everything I could think of that made me angry, sad, or scared. Once that long, tear-stained list was done, I took each one of those items and placed them into a column either "for grieving" or "for reordering." This process helped me bring my grief and confusion before Yahweh. Naming my grief gave me space to feel proper sorrow over the numerous losses caused by this COVID-19 season. The column for reordering (an idea from Augustine's *Confessions*) gave me perspective to see the sins I often love more than the Lord. I was scared because I love my independence, angry because I love control, and anxious because I desire a fruitful career. Like Habakkuk I was upset, wondering how long I would have to endure this sorrowful season.

In some ways Habakkuk was right to be enraged and grieved at the injustice around him. As people who bear the image of God, our desire for justice—for light in the darkness of this world—is a reflection of his image. We are even given a picture of this as Jesus wept in John 11 over the death of his friend and the sorrow it caused. I believe we should grieve and be angry at the pain caused by COVID-19, the loss of work, the sickness and death, the lost joy of graduation and wedding parties. We should wake up each day knowing there will be good moments to celebrate and hard moments to add to our list of losses. But with confident hope, we must remember that neither the rise of the Babylonians nor this pandemic took God by surprise. God did not go on a weekend trip with friends only to come home to find the pandemic had spread beyond his control. In the midst of this collective loss we must, like Habakkuk, remember the faithful love of our Lord, who in all things remains the Rock, salvation, and strength of his people (Hab. 3:18–19; Ps. 40; John 10:18; Phil. 2:1–15).

A POTTED PLANT

MOSES Y. LEE

Planting a Multi-ethnic Church in the Time of Corona

———

Moses is the pastor of Rosebrook Presbyterian Church in North Bethesda, Maryland. He earned degrees from the University of Maryland (BS) and Westminster Theological Seminary (MDiv, ThM). He writes for The Gospel Coalition *and the* SOLA Network. *He is married to Rachel, and they have the joy of raising their son, a fifth-generation Presbyterian.*

———

"Go plant a church," they said. "It'll be fun," they said.

My wife and I had unknowingly planned to gather people for our church plant and launch our first service during one of the worst times to plant a church in modern history. When I started my church planting apprenticeship in October of 2019, I had no way of knowing a global pandemic would practically shutdown the entire world by March of 2020. Of all the worst-case scenarios I could've imagined enduring through my apprenticeship, this wasn't one of them.

Our first setback was cancelling all in-person gatherings, Bible studies, and interest meetings because of the lockdown. We had to stop all in-person recruitment and resort to texting, emailing, and Facebook messaging to invite people to our Zoom Bible studies and fellowship activities. As an extrovert, I constantly wrestled with depression. I needed to see my flock. I needed to hug them. I needed to cry with them. As a perfectionist, I was so frustrated by the cyber barrier that artificially kept us from truly connecting. Oh, then my laptop died a few weeks later.

Just when I thought it couldn't get any worse, the FBI acknowledged an increasing number of racist attacks against Asian Americans, with people blaming us for the devastation the pandemic has caused. *Shit. Is this really happening?*

Things with some of our non-Asian neighbors got weird from there. During one afternoon during the lockdown, my wife went out for a walk with our infant son and dog and she forgot her mask. On her way back home, a white male neighbor yelled at her, expressing his frustration and disgust at her for not wearing a mask despite her maintaining proper social distancing. She came home startled and shaken up. We were pissed off. We were scared for our son. *Are these really the people that God has called us to serve?*

To top it all off, we received back-to-back emails from two of our most generous supporters. They both lost their jobs within the same week, and their giving would cease immediately. We would now have to survive the lockdown with a significant pay cut. Then my wife was told by her boss that the non-profit she worked for was relocating from Washington, DC, to Boston in two months. If she wanted to keep her job and health insurance, we would have to move to Boston with the non-profit. *God, are you telling us not to plant this church?*

I knew full well that church planting would be difficult. I've read the books. I've heard the stories. I even tried to suppress the desire to plant for several years until I couldn't keep it bottled up anymore. But never in my wildest imagination did I think it would look like this.

To say my wife and I have wrestled with bouts of anxiety and doubt would be an understatement. Yet, through it all, God was quietly moving. He was working behind the scenes. He was exposing idols in our hearts and leading us to the cross. He was removing anything and everything that might be a distraction from completely depending on him to plant this church. He was giving us a vision of what our church plant could look like.

A Journey through Fire

When I think about the last ministry my wife and I left and where we're headed with our church plant, I think of Lot's wife after the destruction of Sodom by fire. After Lot and his family left Sodom, they couldn't go back to their former lives. Their future was unclear and they weren't sure what God had planned for them next. But Lot's wife looked back, longing for her previous life, unsure of where God was taking them next, and we know the rest of the story.

My wife and I left our previous ministry on good terms, but we were exhausted from being the only family of color on staff. We needed a break, but we also needed time to reflect and repent. In many ways, my wife and I continue to wrestle with the tension that Lot and his family wrestled with. We can't go back, but we're not sure where God is exactly taking us either. Yet one thing's for certain. God is purifying us by fire from the idols we brought with us from our previous ministry—idols of comfort, financial security, cultural assimilation, self-righteousness, and the American dream. I'm reminded of the following words from the Apostle Peter:

In this you rejoice, though now for a little while, if necessary, you have been grieved by various trials, so that the tested genuineness of your faith—more precious than gold that perishes though it is tested by fire—may be found to result in praise and glory and honor at the revelation of Jesus Christ. Though you have not seen him, you love him. Though you do not now see him, you believe in him and rejoice with joy that is inexpressible and filled with glory, obtaining the outcome of your faith, the salvation of your souls.
(1 Pet. 1:6–9)

In that sense, we have to believe that these trials are actually good for us whether we end up planting a church or not.

So we can't look back. And in the time of Corona, we don't even have the luxury of looking back. We must continue to look forward to the trials he has in store for us because it's only when we see the idols of our hearts that our Savior becomes dearer to us. It's when we fall flat on our faces due to our sin and weakness—not when we're standing tall and proud of what we know or what we've accomplished—that we have nowhere else to look but to the Savior who lived the perfect life we couldn't live and died the death we deserved on our behalf.

I have to remind myself of this everyday as a church planter, especially in the time of Corona.

In an interview conducted by an American pastor about how American churches can be praying for North Korean Christians, one underground North Korean pastor said, "You pray for us? We pray for you! That's the problem with you American Christians and South Korean Christians! You have so much, you put your faith in your money and in your freedom. In North Korea we have neither money nor freedom, but we have Christ, and we've found he's sufficient."[1]

Indeed, we can't truly know Jesus is all we need until Jesus is all we have. Are we ready to lose everything, including our ministries, during this season and still proclaim, "Jesus is sufficient"? *God, I hope so.*

A Renewed Conviction for Unity and Diversity

When my wife and I first started praying about church planting, one of the first things we got excited about was the opportunity to create a worship space for people of color led by Christians of color.

But we knew the reality that people tend to follow people that look like them so we were fully ready to lead an Asian American majority church. After all, the Asian American community is incredibly diverse and multi-ethnic in itself. In fact, I always found it odd that when a church was 80 percent white and 20 percent other, people would call it a multiethnic church, but when a church was 80 percent pan-Asian and 20 percent other, the same people would call it an Asian American church. Why the double standard?

We also felt a strong conviction to create a space that welcomed our Black and Brown brothers and sisters. But knowing the complicated history between the Black and Asian American communities, we knew this would be a challenge and would require contextualized discipleship for our Asian American brothers and sisters in order to help them understand issues pertaining to systemic racism, the model minority myth, etc.

Providentially, the rise of anti-Asian racism in the midst of COVID-19 provided the perfect discipleship opportunity to teach empathy for and reconciliation with our Black neighbors and Black core team members. For the first time since the abolishment of the Chinese Exclusion Act in 1965, Asian Americans were experiencing racism on a collective scale we haven't seen since the civil rights movement. For the first time in a long time, Asian Americans felt unsafe while doing everyday things like grocery shopping, going on a walk or jog, etc. We got a tiny taste of what it's like to be Black in America.

In one sense, these discipleship opportunities over Zoom were invaluable. Our privileged Asian American core team members were starting to get it. Then the video of Ahmaud Arbery's murder was leaked to the public and we immediately had to put into practice what we've been learning. We lamented as a core team. We prayed. And we lamented some more. We put into practice 1 Corinthians 12:26: *"If one member suffers, all suffer together."*

I then had the opportunity to remind our Asian American core team members, "Now imagine feeling unsafe in public spaces from the moment you're born, day after day, with the justice system, financial system, and education system all working against you. And we wonder why people are protesting on the streets. Asian Americans have protested for far less. We need to do better." And we wept together over Zoom.

A Biblical Theological Vision for Flourishing

As a church planter trying to make sense of what God was trying to do in our small community, frankly, I was a bit dumbfounded by what was going on at a national level. The politically divisive rhetoric, the conspiracy theories, and the protests over personal liberties stood as such a stark contrast to how my motherland, South Korea, was handling the pandemic. But if I couldn't tell our nation's leaders how to do their jobs, I knew at least I had to wisely shepherd the small flock the Lord has entrusted me. But how?

One morning in early May, I was spending some personal time in the Psalms when I felt a strong urge to meditate on the leadership of Joseph as vice-regent of Egypt. Now, I'm not one to believe in the continuation of the revelatory gifts, but, almost in an instant, I felt like my heart got flooded with a wave of Christotelic revelation. And then it hit me.

Joseph's appointment by Pharaoh as the vice-regent of Egypt (Gen. 41:40) is an intermittent Adamic fulfillment of the First Adam's enthronement over the earth as Yahweh's vice-regent (Gen. 1:28). But just like Adam capitulated his role as vice-regent, Joseph's rule was imperfect in that his authority derived from a foreign king with false claims to godhood. Yet just as Joseph derived his authority from one greater than himself and ruled with divine authority as a representative and intercessor between the divine and his people, Jesus, the Last Adam (Rom. 5:12-21, 1 Cor. 15:45), derives his authority from one greater than himself (Matt. 28:18) and rules with authority as a divine representative and intercessor (Heb. 7:25) between the true God and his people. Thus, Joseph's imperfect vice-regency was ultimately pointing to Jesus' perfect vice-regency where he rules from his seat at the right of God the Father (Acts 7:55-56).

Likewise, Joseph's reign over a flourishing Egypt was ultimately pointing to Christ's reign over a flourishing cosmic, garden-temple (Eph. 2:19–22) which we also inherit as co-rulers and co-stewards of the earth (Matt. 5:5). Therefore, to live out our Christian calling as co-rulers and co-stewards entails we pursue flourishing over all the earth (Gen. 41:57), a flourishing marked by generosity (Gen. 45:5), plentiful distribution of basic needs (Gen. 41:56), and preparation for future disasters (Gen. 41:53–54). In other words, cosmic flourishing demands wise leadership, a leadership that heals old wounds (Gen. 45:1–4), gathers the poor and the hungry (Gen. 45:11), and makes room for sojourners, refugees, and immigrants (Gen. 41:56–57; 46:5).

I had to repent. First, Jesus is the flawless vice-regent who rules over our world with perfect wisdom. He's generous to all people (especially his own), prepared for this pandemic, and heals old wounds in the midst of great calamity. Second, I started letting go of thinking about what we didn't have and started to ask how we can pour out more of ourselves. We may not have much materially, but we have the Kingdom of God (Luke 6:20).

Courage, dear heart.

1. "The Surprising Prayers of North Korea's Christians," *CBN News*, October 28, 2016, **https://www1.cbn.com/cbnnews/cwn/2016/ october/the-surprising-prayers-of-north-koreas-christians**.

STAYING IN AND SPREADING HOPE

LANCE LEWIS

The Church in the Time of Corona

———

Lance serves as a pastor in northern California. He has a BS in Psychology from Temple University and a MATS from Chesapeake Training Center. He is married to Sharon, and they have two adult children.

———

While at the height of its power, the Roman Empire suffered a devastating epidemic in 165 AD that would ultimately contribute to its decline. Based on historical accounts of the symptoms, modern researchers believe the empire was afflicted with a widespread outbreak of smallpox.

The smallpox epidemic significantly impacted every aspect of Roman society, including its military, economy, agriculture, and religion. One of the lasting effects of the epidemic was the spread of Christianity throughout the empire. Christianity took hold even though it was a relatively new faith with a somewhat odd and auspicious beginning. Moreover, it grew in spite of long-standing persecution.

The following account sheds a bit of light on how and why Christianity spread even as faith in the ancient Roman Pantheon waned.

John Horgan sets the stage for us in an article he wrote for the Ancient History Encyclopedia. He writes:

> The effect of the illness was not confined to the military and economy. Marcus Aurelius launched persecutions against Christians who refused to pay homage to the gods, which, the emperor believed, in turn angered the gods whose wrath made itself known in the form of a devastating epidemic. Ironically the anti-Christian attacks produced the opposite effect amongst the general population.
>
> Unlike adherents to the Roman polytheistic system, Christians believed in an obligation to assist others in a time of need, including illness. Christians were willing to provide the most basic needs, food and water, for those too ill to fend for themselves. This simple level of nursing care produced good feelings between Christians and their pagan neighbors. Christians often stayed to provide assistance while pagans fled. Furthermore,Christianity provided meaning to life and death in times of crisis. Those who survived gained comfort in knowing that loved ones, who died as Christians, could receive the reward of heaven. The Christian promise of salvation in the afterlife attracted additional followers, thus expanding the growth of monotheism within a polytheistic culture. The gaining of adherents established the context in which Christianity would emerge as the sole, official religion of the empire."[1]

In many ways, the ancient church fulfilled the role of our modern-day nurses, nurses' aids, EMTs, and other medical servants. They risked their lives to provide care and comfort to the suffering despite being the objects of official government hostility.

Why did the church respond in this manner, and what lessons can we take from its response?

The ancient church held firmly to a life-altering faith in the identity, teaching, lifestyle, and promise of our Lord Jesus Christ. I'll explore each of these aspects of their faith to answer the questions concerning their response and how it can impact ours during and beyond the Covid-19 pandemic.

Identity

Our identity defines who we are which in turn explains why we exist. Ancient believers fully identified with the person, work, and rule of our Lord Jesus Christ. Their belief in Christ profoundly shaped how they viewed themselves as Roman citizens. Consequently, they no longer felt the pull to lean on their Roman identity as the primary means through which they'd access a life of meaning, purpose, importance, hope, and security. Ancient believers didn't live for the greatness of the Roman Empire. Nor did they find their identity, and ultimate well-being, in a secure and prosperous Rome.

Passages like Daniel 7:13–14 encouraged ancient believers to ground their hope in the eternal kingdom of the living God, ruled by the Lord Jesus Christ. Daniel writes:

> *I saw in the night visions, and behold, with the clouds of heaven there came one like a son of man, and he came to the Ancient of Days and was presented before him. And to him was given dominion and glory and a kingdom, that all peoples, nations, and languages should serve him; his dominion is an everlasting dominion, which shall not pass away, and his kingdom one that shall not be destroyed.* (Dan. 7:13–14)

They were convinced Christ's kingdom was far more

beautiful, far more precious, far more righteous, far more just, and that it would flourish throughout eternity long after the Roman Empire fell to ruin.

Their firm belief in Christ and his kingdom meant they didn't retreat from their society in the face of catastrophic disease accompanied by fierce persecution. The certainty of their place in the new heaven and new earth motivated them to diligently obey Christ's teaching concerning the character of his kingdom.

Teaching

In the gospels, Christ's teaching focused on the Kingdom of God. The Sermon on the Mount highlights the character of those who comprise the kingdom. It stresses the values for which his followers would be known. Eschewing the arrogant, greedy, and self-centered character of the religious leaders of his time, our Lord taught his followers to cultivate selflessness, service, and sacrifice. Instead of believing themselves to be morally superior to others, they were to view themselves as servants to those in need. Matthew 5:13–16 aptly summarized their attitude throughout the epidemic:

> *You are the salt of the earth, but if salt has lost its taste, how shall its saltiness be restored? It is no longer good for anything except to be thrown out and trampled under people's feet. You are the light of the world. A city set on a hill cannot be hidden. Nor do people light a lamp and put it under a basket, but on a stand, and it gives light to all in the house. In the same way, let your light shine before others, so that they may see your good works and give glory to your Father who is in heaven.* (Matt. 5:13–16)

Propelled by Christ's teaching, our ancient brothers and sisters took it upon themselves to become Rome's nursing corps throughout the epidemic.

Lifestyle

Jesus practiced what he preached. He went throughout the countryside of ancient Palestine regularly healing the sick and tending to the needs of the vulnerable. Observing his way of life provided Christ's earliest followers with a powerful example of how his people should live within any society.

Jesus once called attention to his way of life in response to a question about his identity with these words:

> And Jesus answered them, Go and tell John what you hear and see: the blind receive their sight and the lame walk, lepers are cleansed and the deaf hear, and the dead are raised up, and the poor have good news preached to them. And blessed is the one who is not offended by me. (Matt. 11:4–6)

When the Antione epidemic began to rip through the Roman Empire, Christ's followers continued their mission of proclaiming his message of forgiveness and universal rule. They did so by imitating the lifestyle of their Lord by doing good, providing care, and spreading hope.

Promise

As the Ancient History Encyclopedia article related, God's people drew comfort from their hope in the afterlife as they threw themselves into caring for the sick and dying. Jesus spoke of this hope throughout the gospels and secured it by his sinless life, sacrificial death, and bodily resurrection from the grave. Believers obtain this guarantee of an afterlife in the new heavens and earth through faith alone in Christ's finished work.

Their hope in Christ impacted the ancient church's service during the epidemic in at least three ways. First, armed with the certainty of eternal, physical life on a new earth, God's people were liberated from the innate human drive to achieve ultimate well-being within this lifetime. Second, they replaced the ambition to get the most from this present life, with that of serving their society in a time of need. Third, the ancient church was free to help in this way, knowing their eternal destinies didn't depend on the amount or perfection of their service.

The ancient church didn't throw their lives away needlessly. Instead, emboldened by Christ's guaranteed hope of a new heaven and new earth, they freely served their society in its great time of need.

———

Here are a few lessons the contemporary church in American can draw from our ancient brothers and sisters along the lines of our identity, teaching, lifestyle, and promise.

Identity

But you are a chosen race, a royal priesthood, a holy nation, a people for his own possession, that you may proclaim the excellencies of him who called you out of darkness into his marvelous light. Once you were not a people, but now you are God's people; once you had not received mercy, but now you have received mercy.
1 Peter 2:9–10

The Apostle Peter accurately distilled the primary identity of God's people. We exist primarily to broadcast his being, character, and saving work to our society. Our central identity is not that of American citizens whose sole focus is protecting our Constitutional rights. God's chief purpose for placing us in America (see 1 Pet. 1:1) has nothing to do with securing our piece of the American dream or obtaining the blessings of liberty. If we fall into the trap of prioritizing our American citizenship over our identity in Christ, we'll most certainly lose our focus and our witness. Living as God's people placed in America empowers us to draw our thirst for overall well-being from who we are in Christ. We can, therefore, witness to those who've tied their identity to America and its way of life.

Teaching

Keep your conduct among the Gentiles honorable, so that when they speak against you as evildoers, they may see your good deeds and
glorify God on the day of visitation.
1 Peter 2:12

The Apostle Peter followed the truth of our true identity by confirming our Lord's teaching. As Jesus taught, the church doesn't use our identity to despise or hide from our society. Instead, we plunge into our communities doing good, helping the needy, and protecting the vulnerable as an ongoing display of God's loving compassion. Following Christ's teaching provides a tangible witness of his message of forgiveness and eternal hope under his rule. It also conveys our genuine concern for those in our society.

Our commitment to obey Christ's teaching calls us to adopt a mindset of service during this pandemic, shaping the way we view those in our society. Consequently, we refuse to see our culture as a battlefield over ideological rights but as a people in need of a shepherd. Moving our worship services to online formats is a prime example of following our Lord's teaching. Meeting online during the pandemic is one of the main ways we can serve our community's basic need for safety. We do so in obedience to Jesus' teaching on the value of life.

Now who is there to harm you if you are zealous for what is good?
But even if you should suffer for righteousness' sake, you will be
blessed.
Have no fear of them, nor be troubled, but in your hearts honor
Christ the Lord as holy, always being prepared to make a
defense to anyone who asks you for a reason for the hope that is
in you;
yet do it with gentleness and respect, having a good conscience,
so that, when you are slandered, those who revile your good
behavior
in Christ may be put to shame. For it is better to suffer for doing
good,
if that should be God's will, than for doing evil. For Christ also
suffered once for sins, the righteous for the unrighteous, that he
might
bring us to God, being put to death in the flesh but made alive in
the spirit.
1 Peter 3:13–18

Throughout 1 Peter, the apostle strongly encouraged God's people to imitate Christ's lifestyle, even if it earned the ire of their society. Peter knew a life devoted to doing good for others could lead to hostility and even death based on his close observation of Christ. He also knew Christ remained committed to a lifestyle of doing good up to the point of his death. One account of our Lord's arrest highlights his commitment to do good even in the face of fierce hostility. Peter was directly involved in the incident, which I believed shaped his future outlook on our witness in the presence of conflict.

Luke's gospel (chapter 22) relates the account of Jesus healing the ear one of those who came to arrest him. The Apostle John identified Peter as the man's attacker (John 18) who sliced off his ear while going for his head. Jesus immediately commanded Peter to put away his sword and then restored the man's ear (Luke 22:51).

Peter may have learned a valuable lesson that night. A lifestyle of good works propels the Kingdom of God and the message it proclaims. God hasn't called us to scold, shun, and pick fights with our society. Embracing the lifestyle of Jesus, characterized by good works, is in stark contrast to a culture that so treasures its individualized rights, comfort, convenience, and me-first, me-only attitude.

It's the way of life practiced by the ancient church in response to one of the gravest times in human history. Despite having to care for their own sick, the church followed the lifestyle of Jesus, loved their community, and, in doing so, pointed them to Christ's promise.

Promise

Blessed be the God and Father of our Lord Jesus Christ! According to
his great mercy, he has caused us to be born again to a living hope through the resurrection of Jesus Christ from the dead, to an inheritance
that is imperishable, undefiled, and unfading, kept in heaven for you,
who by God's power are being guarded through faith for a salvation
ready to be revealed in the last time. In this you rejoice, though now for a
little while, if necessary, you have been grieved by various trials.
1 Peter 1:3–6

Peter kicked off his letter with a breathtaking declaration of the unique promise of our full and final salvation through faith in Jesus Christ. Christ's promise provided a complete and sure hope while at the same time preparing God's people for the inevitable hardships of persecution.

Christ's blessed hope is the source of our genuine delight, despite suffering because of our faith. Our hope frees us from depending on America to deliver the fruits of the good life if we just work hard and have the right political leaders in place. Especially during this pandemic, our hope serves as a strong defense to the sinking feeling American society may never be the same.

Our hope is precisely what our world in general and America in particular needs. However our current crisis ends, most of us don't believe it will be our last crisis. What will the next one bring, and how will it chip away at the already frayed strands of our society? Americans are experiencing sharp increases in emotional, psychological, and social distress. Our society is adrift, and we're not likely to get back to normal any time soon. COVID-19 has pulled back the curtain and revealed our idolatry of the United States of America. It's exposed America for what it is; an empty, flawed, broken, and rebellious society that can in no way fulfill the hope of those who look to her for their ultimate sense of well-being.

Americans needs a true savior who guarantees authentic hope. And by the grace of the living God, we are the people blessed and privileged to bring it to them.

---

1. *Ancient History Encyclopedia* s.v. "Antonine Plague" published May 2, 2019, https://www.ancient.eu/Antonine_Plague/

HOPE IN THE TIME OF CORONA

NO MAN IS AN ISLAND

JEREMY FAIR

Margaritas in the Time of Corona

———

Jeremy is the Senior Pastor of Christ Presbyterian Church in Tulsa, Oklahoma. He holds a BA in Religion and Philosophy from Dallas Baptist University, an MDiv from Southwestern Baptist Theological Seminary, and a DMin from Knox Theological Seminary. Prior to serving in Tulsa, Jeremy served churches in Texas and Alabama. He is married to Kimbo, and they have three sons and a daughter. He is also a second-generation member of the Tulsa Parrot Head Club.

The margarita is the cocktail of dive bar slushie machines and tourists visiting Cabo San Lucas—or so we are led to believe. Yet it actually has a rich history dating to the middle of the twentieth century and has experienced a recent resurgence among craft mixologists.

Like many classic cocktails, the origin of the margarita is debated. Some claim that it was the creation of Margaret Sames, a Texas socialite who mixed it up for her friends on a Mexican vacation in 1948. Others claim that it was created for actress Rita Hayworth (Hayworth's given name was Margarita Cansino) by an admiring bartender in the mid 1940s. Still others claim that it is a celebratory cocktail created in honor of Saint Margaret of Cortona, a Franciscan nun who devoted her life to Christ in the thirteenth century. According to historian David Wondrich, author of *Imbibe!*, the most likely origin is that the margarita evolved from a cocktail known as the "daisy," a popular drink during the 1930s and 40s. At some point, the Mexican-influenced daisy became known by its Spanish name, margarita, which means daisy in Spanish. Whatever the true origin of the margarita may be, it has remained a staple of warm weather imbibing for nearly eighty years.

At its worst, the margarita is a haphazard blend of ingredients paired with unending tortilla chips and salsa. At its best, it is a liquid celebration of life and the joys of warm weather. Visions of margaritas transport us to sandy beaches, seasonal celebrations, and gatherings of friends with the common desire to *carpe diem*. When you think of a margarita, do not call to mind a careless combination of tequila and some prepackaged mixture. Instead envision a carefully crafted cocktail that combines the flavors of citrus and salt, a thoughtful blend of tequila, lime, triple sec, and as many flavor variations as the mind of the maker allows.

When selecting ingredients in the store, rather than thoughtlessly taking hold of a bottle of tequila from a lower shelf with a label that is easily recognizable, move your eyes to the lesser known but flavor-rich offerings on the upper shelves. A good tequila need not be expensive. It must, however, be 100 percent blue agave and originate in Jalisco, Mexico. I recommend a *reposado* that has been aged for at least six months.

Nearly as important as the choice of tequila is the choice of triple sec orange liqueur. Steer clear of the overly syrupy generic brands and you will experience a notably superior taste. Many people enjoy the added flavors of strawberry, mango, apple, or watermelon. I prefer the traditional flavors of citrus and salt that come out in simplicity from the basic ingredients.

During the coronavirus pandemic many people have turned to alcohol as an escape from the harsh realities of daily life. The workday ends with several fingers of whiskey or a few adjunct lagers to numb the pain. Social distancing has relegated drinking to a lonely exercise, less about celebration and more about isolation. The margarita, however, stands in defiance to escapism and purposeless pain—its very nature cries out for community and intentionality.

A margarita is meant to be a shared drink. It is meant to be enjoyed among friends and to highlight joy in the moment. This raises the interesting questions: Does the margarita have a place in the time of Corona? Can it rightly be enjoyed in a time of so much pain and loss?

I believe it does and it can. In the midst of a season when we appropriately mourn and lament, there is an equally appropriate time to celebrate. In a season when we must necessarily maintain social distance, there is a desperate need to maintain social connections.

I've often told my wife that if I weren't a pastor, I'd like to be a bartender. This desire comes from no special affinity for alcohol but from a desire to display creativity and extend compassion to patrons in the shared moments of life. A bartender possesses many of the same qualities as a pastor and fulfills a similar role: a listening ear; a confidant; perhaps a phone call to get you home. They both speak a word of good news into the ever-present bad news.

On one particular afternoon, about five weeks into the season of social distancing, I participated in a Zoom call with some friends and colleagues. This was a group of men who have been as close as brothers, and we recognized the need for connection and camaraderie. The call was set for happy hour and the understanding was that the participants would bring a "shared" drink to the virtual gathering. Most of my brothers brought a beer or a glass of whiskey.

I brought a carefully crafted margarita. To complement my margarita, I donned a tropical shirt and sat in the sunlight that draped my front porch. My attire and choice of drink were both an act of defiance and an act of celebration. *Stick it, Corona! Here's to hope in the future!*

The Psalmist tells us that our gracious God has given us *"wine to gladden the heart of man"* (Ps. 104:15). Far from a utilitarian activity, enjoying a margarita with friends is a gladdening experience. Taking the time to carefully select and prepare the ingredients is an exercise in creativity born of the *imago Dei*. Instead of seeking an escape from the harsh realities of my present situation, the enjoyment of a margarita held out the promise of hope—one day, in the not too distant future, the summer sun will shine with warmth and light as a reminder that the light has come into the darkness and we are meant to bask in the light together.

Recipes

Traditional
1 ½ oz. tequila
¾ oz. lime juice
½ oz. triple sec
1 lime wedge for garnish

Pour ingredients into a shaker filled with ice and shake forty times. Strain into an 8 oz. margarita glass rimmed with coarse salt.

Island Time (Personal Favorite)
3 oz. reposado tequila
2 oz. lime juice
1 oz. Gran Gala

½ oz. agave nectar
1 oz. Topo Chico

Coat the rim of an 8 oz. margarita glass with Tajín. Pour ingredients except Topo Chico into a shaker filled with ice and shake forty times. Strain into a glass filled with ice and add a 1 oz. splash of Topo Chico.

Frozen
6 oz. reposado tequila
6 oz. Minute Maid frozen limeade concentrate
2 oz. Gran Gala
½ oz. blue curaçao

Pour all ingredients except blue curaçao into a blender and add two cups of cubed ice. Blend for sixty seconds. Pour 8 oz. of blended margarita into a rocks glass and carefully pour ½ oz. blue curaçao down the inside of the glass as a "sinking floater."

———

God's gifts are meant to be enjoyed but not abused. If you think you may have a problem with enjoying alcohol in moderation, ask for help.

SENSING REDEMPTION
MARK GRAPENGATER

**Finding Beauty to Save the Soul
in the Time of Corona**

———

*Mark is a pastor and church planter at The Table Project in
Denver, Colorado. He has a degree in Spanish from Kansas State
University (BA) and received an MDiv from North Park Theolog-
ical Seminary. He has previously served in churches in Chicago,
Illinois, St. Louis, Missouri, and Decatur, Georgia. He is married
to Stacey, and they have three children.*

———

If I had an orchard, I'd work till I'm sore.
Fleet Foxes, *Helplessness Blues*[1]

Beauty will save the world.
Fyodor Dostoevsky, *The Idiot*[2]

I was on my regular walk around our neighborhood in
Southeast Denver. The arhythmic rollercoaster of quaran-

tine life, homeschooling our kindergartner, and lack of social interaction were weighing heavy on me. Adding to that weight was the severe lack of sleep due to our four-week-old son for whom rhythm was a foreign concept. It was April, and although spring was in the air, it was dense and oppressive.

Questions and longings plagued my mind. *How long was this going to last? When will it end? When can we fill our house with friends and laughter again?*

I kept wondering what else I needed to make it through the time of Corona. *Why do I feel so depressed? What is lacking?*

Heading home, it hit me—I needed beauty. I needed some sense of redemption to break through to remind me that this is only a season. I needed someone to speak, paint, color, sing, grow, and plate something that wrestled with the range of emotions that weighed so heavily on me.

Being told to stay at home in Colorado is incredibly challenging. Thousands of people move to Denver each month just to be near the mountains, to be able to look out over the crest of an urban hill and see the grandeur of the Rockies on a daily basis. Even if it's just on your daily commute on I-25, the mountains are never more than a thirty-minute detour away. Just having the beauty of the mountains there lifts your heart. Sheltering in our suburban home with our children, we miss that daily experience of beauty.

So I prayed.

"Lord, I need beauty. I need to see that you are moving and working in this wild world. I need to see beyond my circumstances to know that faith, hope, and love are still the governing principles of your kingdom. Help me to taste and see that you are good."

No "Amen" this time. I needed it to hang there like a toddler who will not let go of the need for their parent's intervention.

Beauty has the ability to penetrate deeper than the

function of a thing. It doesn't affect your bones, it affects your soul. Beauty stirs up, tips over, pokes, prods, unearths and discovers the deeper things that often get pushed to the bottom of our hearts as we run the rat race of life. Beauty causes us to pause. Beauty reminds us that things are not the way they are supposed to be. God created you to reflect his beauty. God created us to reveal the glory of our Creator, not simply to produce. Humans were made in the likeness of God to share his likeness with others. The desire for beauty is in us, because God created us beautiful. God is just as concerned with form as he is function.

Beauty Given

By the grace of God, this coronavirus and the subsequent quarantine have taken place in the spring rather than winter. The first beauty I noticed after my desperate prayer was the landscaping. Our neighborhood is on the suburban edge of the city, and people take pride in their yards. The din of lawn mowers echo through quiet, cool mornings. Without work responsibilities, people were getting a jump on their gardens—raking, weeding, planting, and mulching. Tulips, foxgloves, phlox, and daffodils were making their first appearances. The death of winter was fading away and a rich kaleidoscope of colors filled the yards. Bright blues, pinks, yellows, purples and fuchsias were anchored by a sea of green grass perfect for a picnic or a long nap. It was beautiful, and I soaked in all of it.

Many people are returning to gardening this year. Victory gardens, kitchen gardens, balconies, and windowsills are filled with beautiful, and often edible, flowers, herbs, vegetables, and fruit. Masked shoppers are picking through the arrangements at grocery stores and markets. God made all this beautiful. And in the time of Corona, we long for it.

I long for it.

I needed to get my hands in the soil. I needed to create something beautiful.

The previous owners of our house left a wheelbarrow in the corner of the yard. The front wheel was falling off. It was well-rusted. It was perfect. My son and I pulled it to a prominent place in our yard and secured it to the ground. Then we filled it with rich, organic soil, strawberries, parsley, sage, and rosemary. As we mulched over the soil, I stepped back to admire how a useless, old, rusted-out wheel barrow had been transformed into a thing of beauty.

Every day I go out into my yard and tend the plants in that wheel barrow. I pick parsley for my omelettes. I check on the strawberries. It lifts my heart. It gives me hope, which is what I think beauty does.

God doesn't just give us gifts for ourselves though. It's always meant to be shared. If I needed beauty to lift my heart, I was sure other people did also.

Beauty Shared

The Wednesday before Palm Sunday, Denver was glorious. Temperatures were in the mid–70s, the sun was shining, and people were walking. It was like living on a parade route. *There has to be an opportunity to share beauty with all these people,* I thought to myself.

A few years ago, I was introduced to the artist Scott Erickson through his art in a book called *Prayer: Forty Days of Practice.*[3] His images are deep with meaning. Scott has also created two series of images specifically for Holy Week. The first is the *Seven Last Sayings of Jesus*[4] and the second is his take on the traditional Stations of the Cross which he calls *Stations in the Street.*[5]

Stations in the Street walk you through Jesus' last hours from his temptation in the garden to his resurrection on Easter morning. Scott designed it as street art, to be printed in large format and pasted to sidewalks, sides of buildings, and public spaces. As I watched my neighbors walking by, I thought, *This is it. This is how I share beauty with this neighborhood.*

I downloaded the images, printed them three-feet by four-feet, and watched YouTube videos on how to make wheat paste. I texted some neighbors. "Can I paste some really big images about Jesus on the sidewalk in front of your house this next week?" Much to my surprise, the responses I got were a resounding "Yes," even from the non-Christians—"Do your thing." I made the wheat paste and gathered my prints. I felt very punk. All along the sidewalks I put down these massive posters with snakes, chalices, thorns, nails, and lambs cut-in-half. I even printed up a guide with a map and reflection questions for people to take with them if they wanted to use it as a pilgrimage.

We had two outside our house. Individuals, couples, and families stopped and read the long introduction and pondered Jesus' temptation. One mom was with her five-year-old. "I'm trying to explain to her what temptation means." "Hmm," I thought. I love trying to explain things to kids. You have to make it real to them. "Have you ever wanted to do something your mom told you not to?" "Yes," she sheepishly replied, as she looked knowingly at her mom. "That's temptation." "That's a good definition," replied the mom with genuine gratitude in her voice.

It was these images portraying the beauty of Jesus' last days that caused people to stop and ponder something that stirs their souls whether or not they have faith in Jesus. Like the beauty of the garden, these images lifted their spirits.

Beauty sows hope in our souls.

As seedlings poke their first leaves through the soil and early spring flowers open their blossoms to the morning sun, as we lose ourselves in images pasted onto sidewalks, we are given hope. Hope that new life is springing forth. Hope that God is still at work upholding the world. Hope that healing will come. Hope that the season of Corona will have an end. Hope that God will redeem this time—not to return us to "normal" but to redeem us and bring about a more brilliant and more beautiful reflection of who he is in our humanity.

I still don't know when this time of crisis will end, or when my house will be filled with friends and laughter, but I do know this—I don't have to wait for beauty. It's all around me, even in the time of Corona. And I need it now more than ever.

---

1. Fleet Foxes, "Helplessness Blues," 2010, by Robin Pecknold, track 6, on *Helplessness Blues* (Seattle: Sub Pop), 2011, compact disc.
2. Fyodor Dostoevsky, *The Idiot*, trans. Richard Pevear and Larissa Volokhonsky (New Your: Vintage, 2003), 382.
3. Justin McRoberts and Scott Erickson, *Prayer: Forty Days of Practice*, (Colorado Springs: WaterBrook, 2019).
4. Scott Erickson, *Seven Last Sayings of Jesus*, Portland, Scott Erickson Art Shop. https://scottericksonartshop.com/products/seven-last-sayings-of-jesus-downloadable-artwork.
5. Scott Erickson, *Stations in the Street*, Portland, Scott Erickson Art Shop. https://scottericksonartshop.com/collections/stations-in-the-street.

SOUL FOOD
JASON BOBO

God Feeds His People in the Time of Corona

————

Jason is Associate Pastor of Christ Presbyterian Church in Tulsa, Oklahoma. He has degrees from Grand Canyon University (BA) and Westminster Theological Seminary (MDiv). He is married to Tiffany, and they have four children.

————

The liturgy of barbecue is, for me, a life-giving practice. The work of selecting the wood, collecting the meat, blending the concoction of spices, rising before the sun, and babying the fire to keep it right where I want is a labor of love. I get a little stir crazy if I go more than a few weeks without it. I have stacks of books on the history of the cooking method, the collision of ethnicities involved in its evolution, regional preferences, and recipes. Ten years ago, I spent a month researching heat retention and smoke distribution as I designed and welded my own reverse flow barbecue pit. It was a Valentine's gift for my wife, but the door is too heavy for her to lift. Seriously.

I don't just love the practice of prepping and cooking

for an entire day. I've actually gotten pretty good at it. More people than I can remember have told me it was the best brisket, pulled pork, ribs, turkey, ham, chicken, bacon, or salmon candy they've ever had, and that I should dial it in and compete. While I really appreciate the compliments, I have less than zero interest in food competitions. I'm not mad at the people that compete—I think they're amazing chefs, and I respect their mastery of the craft—but for me, I've come to realize, it is actually less about the meat and more about the whole event.

What I love more than the preparation, even more than the finished product, is being outside, music in the background, cold beer in hand, kids running around the yard, and folks clustered up in lawn chairs. I mill about, listening in, sometimes joining in. I enjoy the quiet, behind-the-scenes stuff. I like the finished product most days, but I most deeply love the cacophony of joy and laughter from my friends and family. In the same way that the tortilla chip, no matter how good, is simply the vehicle to shovel the queso into my mouth, my joy in barbecuing is experiencing the people I love, loving one another.

Before the time of Corona, my backyard wasn't a viable option to smoke in because we're on a hill that slopes away and had very limited patio space. I have to say "had" because since the advent of the 'Rona, my sweet wife of twenty one years has been playing the role of general contractor, and we now have a beautiful flagstone patio and are in the middle of additional decking. (Someone could have contributed a chapter in this book on projects my wife has started around the house since being locked in.) All that to say, for the last four years I've been rolling the smoker out of the garage and into the driveway in my jean shorts and camo Piggly Wiggly shirt to get the job done in my fancy pants gated neighborhood. Basically, all I'm missing is a car up on blocks and a pack of Marlboro Reds to win this round of Redneck Bingo.

Now I don't want to move it to the backyard, but it's for the reason you think.

I used to imagine conversations like this:

"Oh my gosh Becky! Did you see the chubby handsome guy trashing the place up with his big ol' smoker in the driveway? He's gonna bring our home values down."

"I did see him Karen, and I don't think he's that handsome."

(That was a fictional conversation that I pictured a couple of ladies who walk our neighborhood having when I first started smoking in the driveway. No Beckys or Karens were harmed or offended enough to speak with the manager in this scenario.)

People would walk by, give a little side eye or head shake, and move on. Then it became a little more accepted, and folks would stop and visit and ask for a tour of the smoker. That migrated to joking shouts of "Hey, what time's dinner?"

When Corona came to town, I decided I would heed Aragon's challenge to Theoden in the *Two Towers* film, and I rode out to meet her. My way of battling the frustration and loss of communal hope was to plan a neighborhood BBQ. Some of those folks who used to squint at me jumped at the idea of a social distance barbecue block party. We fed 25–30 people. A month later I rented a margarita machine and joined forces with a couple of guys to cook the required fajitas for Cinco De Mayo. This time we had more than fifty folks. I'm convinced that my cooking in the driveway for a few years normalized the idea in people's mind that gathering outside in the street one evening to eat together made perfect sense.

Now I don't want to move it to the backyard because I love my neighbors, and I love the place we are becoming together.

If you could turn this mess into an equation, it might look like this: COVID-19 x isolation + fear of the unknown - normal routines = people starving for affection and connection. The two things I love most about hosting a BBQ (what we at home call Bobo-Que) are the people who come together and enjoy each other, and in my mind there had to be a way for us to be together and still honor the expectations of social distancing.

I have always loved the famous quote of Frederick Buechner, "The place where God calls you to is the place where your deep gladness and the world's deep hunger coincide."[1] According to that theory, the place God called me to was a communal meal enjoyed at a safe distance. Not exactly battling the legions of hell, but closer than you might think.

I've cooked for Presbytery meetings. I once cooked for an Easter fellowship meal for an entire church. As VP for Student Affairs at now-defunct Redeemer Seminary (moment of silence), I hosted monthly barbecues for students and professors. And in my current role as Associate Pastor of my own church, I love to host gatherings for members new and old to grow together. But I had never even once considered using my passion and skills to meet new friends *outside* of a ministry or job setting.

It took a global pandemic for me to realize that I can de-church my cooking and use it in a missional way to bless my neighborhood. It might not be a cup of cold water (Matt. 10:42), but I offered it in his name in hopes he might use it to bless and comfort others.

DC pastor Russ Whitfield and I have been close friends for a long time. We often daydream about starting a multi-ethnic, artisanal, small-batch, pasture-to-plate barbecue restaurant (humorously called Ebony and Ivory) where the space would double as a worship and teaching space for a local church to gather—a church which we of course would pastor. It's a terrible plan because Russ plays too much, and I would non-fatally stab him some-day, but also because he is so much fun to be with that I doubt we would get any work done most days. But it's also kind of brilliant too if you think about it.

Some people who might never darken the door of a traditional church, but who are longing for the affection and connection that Christ supplies, might join a group of people meeting in a barbecue restaurant—especially a group willing to display Christian worship and biblical values in compelling and innovative ways. For them, that might sound like a really cool experience. I doubt it would click with everyone, but I also imagine some folks would be intrigued by a gathering of Christians who add a tasty and tangible value to the community space; a gathering of people who are so passionate and good at their craft that even outside participation feels fulfilling; a gathering of people who don't have to talk about money so much since they generate enough income to pay for the building and give their funds to the mission of serving others.

God, too, loves to feed his people. In the very first chapter of the very first book of the Bible we read *"Behold, I have given you every plant yielding seed that is on the face of all the earth, and every tree with seed in its fruit. You shall have them for food"* (Gen. 1:29). And in the very last chapter of the very last book of the Bible we find him doing it again:

> *Then the angel showed me the river of the water of life, bright as crystal, flowing from the throne of God and of the Lamb through the middle of the street of the city; also, on either side of the river, the tree of life with its twelve kinds of fruit, yielding its fruit each month. The leaves of the tree were for the healing of the nations.* (Rev. 22:1–2)

From the world's first drive-through of manna with a side of rock water in the wilderness (Ex. 16 & 17), to the little boy that got his lunch jacked by the apostle Andrew so that Jesus might multiply his fish and barley loaves at the beginning of John 6, the story of the Bible is the story of God feeding his people. Sometimes it's the morsel of daily bread that sustains us in his mercy, while other times it's a wedding feast of steak and cabernet that overwhelms us in his grace. God feeds his people all through the stories of Scripture.

In John 6:53–58, Jesus, says:

Truly, truly, I say to you, unless you eat the flesh of the Son of Man and drink his blood, you have no life in you. Whoever feeds on my flesh and drinks my blood has eternal life, and I will raise him up on the last day. For my flesh is true food, and my blood is true drink. Whoever feeds on my flesh and drinks my blood abides in me, and I in him. As the living Father sent me, and I live because of the Father, so whoever feeds on me, he also will live because of me. This is the bread that came down from heaven, not like the bread the fathers ate, and died. Whoever feeds on this bread will live forever.

All the bread and barbecue we've ever eaten came to us as a gift of grace to bring us to the place where we might feel hunger and thirst for the body and blood of our Savior—true food and true drink in union with the Father and the Son, made eternally alive by the Spirit. Salvation feels like a feast even though it looks like so much less right now. Right now, it looks like a little corner of bread with half an ounce of boxed wine in the sacrament of communion. Pretty basic. Not something you'd order off the menu of *La Grande Maison de Bernard Magrez* in Bordeaux, but it is the true food and true drink that I long to eat and drink in union with Christ, in fellowship with my friends and family at Christ Presbyterian Church in Tulsa, Oklahoma, and with the universal Church.

God feeds his people in order to bring us into the resurrection life of the Son. He also asks us to feed his sheep as we follow him (John 21:18–19). My barbecue is good, but in the grand scheme of things it's little more than fish and loaves. I hand it over to Jesus by faith, in hope that he'll bless it and multiply it and draw some spiritually hungry beggars to himself, the truest food and drink. To that, I say, "Amen."

BBQ Tips I'm Willing to Share

Buy a few BBQ books and pharisaically follow the directions as if you'll be stoned (not in a good way) for breaking them. Once you've done a recipe with success two to three times, you are deputized to get creative with it. Aaron Franklin's book *Franklin Barbecue*[2] is awesome and so is *Meathead* by Meathead Goldwyn[3]. You'll find lots of science and terrific recipes in both.

My briskets are done at 203, pork at 195. Cook to temp not to time, and plan to let your meat rest in a towel lined ice chest (no ice) for at least an hour to two before you dig in.

Beef loves salt, pork loves sugar, and poultry loves a brine.

You can smoke hotter than you probably think without sacrificing texture. I don't go much higher than 275, but there's no reason to stay down at 225.

Just like with Calvinism, there can often be a cage stage with pit masters young and old. People are always willing to fight about what constitutes true BBQ—logs, pellets, or charcoal, offset vs. green egg, sauce or no sauce, etc. If I made the food and they are arguing, I send them away. If they made the food and they are complaining (and its good), then I agree with them and continuing eating. Just don't fight about good food, OK?

My favorite spritz to both moisten and sweeten the meat, but also add a nice bark, is a 1/4 to 3/4 blend of apple juice and olive oil. I hit it every 45 minutes to an hour with that.

I have saved myself so much frustration by buying
a flame thrower that attaches to a propane tank for
when I'm smoking, and it's cold outside.

One of my family's favorite traditions is coming up
with innovative new dishes for two to three days
after a big BBQ. We love green chile pulled pork
enchiladas and brisket and veggie pastys. I recently
made pulled pork curry that may have changed me
at a cellular level.

---

1. Frederick Buechner, *Wishful Thinking: A Seeker's ABC. Rev. and expanded [ed.]* (San Francisco: Harper SanFrancisco, 1993).
2. Aaron Franklin and Jordan Macay, *Franklin Barbecue: A Meat-Smoking Manifesto* (Berkely: Ten Speed Press, 2015).
3. Meathead Goldwyn and Greg Blonder, *Meathead* (Boston New York: Houghton Mifflin Harcourt, 2016).

TASTING GOD
HYUNG (DAVID) MIN BAE

Eating in the Time of Corona

——————

Hyung (David) is the Worship Pastor at the Korean Presbyterian Church of Washington in Fairfax, Virginia. He was born in Seoul, South Korea, and raised in Northern Virginia. He has an MDiv from Westminster Theological Seminary and is an ordained minister in the Presbyterian Church in America (PCA). In addition to serving as a pastor, Hyung owns and operates an Asian American-inspired cafe in Washington DC.

——————

I spend a lot of time thinking about food. I'm constantly asking myself questions: "How does this taste? Why does it taste that way? How does it feel? How will it be ten minutes from now?" I also tend to process my thoughts verbally. As you might imagine, I am very fun on dinner dates (though it's often insisted otherwise). Call it a personal passion or an occupational hazard, but once I start thinking about food, it's hard to stop.

That's not to say I'm dispassionate about pastoral ministry. I love being a pastor. It is such a privilege and joy to preach the Gospel and help people apply it to the ins-and-outs of their lives. But I also have the unique privilege of making ice cream for a living. I run a small cafe that specializes in East Asian styles of tea and makes East Asian inspired flavors of ice cream. We're constantly changing our menu—bringing back old favorites, while also introducing new tastes. On warm days, I can see groups of friends, families, co-workers, and romantic interests all around my cafe, laughing, enjoying the weather, and bonding over our ice cream.

I miss those days. The good 'ole days that people talk about. You know, those days when two friends sharing an ice cream wasn't a reckless health risk? Those days when you didn't have a mask to take off before eating? Those days when we saw others as sources of potential joy rather than potential risk and danger.

Between all the stay-at-home orders, fears of infection, and transmission of COVID-19, it feels like we've lost a lot of the good things we used to enjoy. Sports have been cancelled, restaurants shut down, and worship relegated to the other side of a screen. This pandemic has robbed us of so much that we enjoy. I have no doubt that you lost some good in your life due to the outbreak. We all have. But you know what has remained intact through all this?

How good food is.

I'm not trying to be flippant, or make light of a terrible and difficult situation, but do you know what I taste when I eat something good? I taste God's goodness. Do you know what I see when I serve a person something good? I see the goodness of God. The realities of our circumstances have hindered our connection with so many of the ways that we traditionally experience God's goodness. Community, good health, and even worship at church has been significantly affected. But the psalmist invites us to *"taste and see that the LORD is good"* (Ps. 34:8), and maybe this whole tasting and seeing business is a little less metaphorical than we thought. Maybe tasting and seeing has a little less to do with our *thoughts*, and a little more to do with our *tongues*.

Isn't the LORD so good to us that when he feeds us, he makes it taste *good*? I find it amazing that God concerns himself not only with the *sufficiency* of the food on our table, but also the *flavor* of it. I am convinced that God loves delicious things, and as ones made in his image, it is only right and natural for us to love and find joy in delicious things too. Isn't God so good to us that eating is not simply a necessity of life, but rather a joyous activity? Isn't this the form of worship that for so many of us, most naturally blends duty with delight? God is surely good to us.

Not as many people come to the cafe as they used to. But you know what? People still come. They come in their cars, on their bicycles, and with their dogs. Some live nearby, and others drive for almost an hour. And sometimes they say, "This is so *good*."

It's in those moments I am reminded that the goodness of God is found not only in our prayers and on our pages, but also on our tables and in our hands. We can enjoy the goodness of God not just with our *souls* but also with our *stomachs*.

How can we give God glory in these uncertain times? We can eat good things, make good things, and serve good things. Our circumstances may have robbed us of so much that is good, but God's goodness endures. Our condition may be bitter, but we can taste God's goodness even now. So, let's roll up our sleeves, grab our spoons, and get some ice cream[1]. One for ourselves, and another for our neighbors. I'll see you at the table.

---

1. Or whatever you find delicious. Personally, this writer also enjoys pasta, noodles, and whiskey.

WAITING FOR GOD
ROB WOOTTON

Waiting Well in the Time of Corona

———

Rob is a church planter in Billings, Montana. He has a BFA in Art Education from Virginia Commonwealth University and an MDiv from Covenant Theological Seminary. Rob is married to Robin, and they have four children.

———

There's a scene in the movie *National Treasure* where the three main characters are in a car with the guy who provides the comic relief in the back seat. This character, Riley, says, "Are we there yet? I'm hungry. This car smells funny."

After seeing the movie years ago, when my older kids were young, this line got repeated over and over again. Inevitably a child from the backseat of a car would say, "Are we there yet?" To which I would always reply, "I'm hungry. This car smells funny." It annoyed them at first, but since they liked the movie and thought it was funny, they would quickly understand that I was correcting their struggle to wait.

We all have that struggle. We don't like to wait. I think it's particularly true for us in our American culture of excess, but it's a human condition. Many songs were written about waiting on God that are recorded in the Psalms. There are other stories of waiting on the Lord throughout the Bible. Like many of the struggles of our fallen and broken human condition, God speaks directly and often clearly to our inability to wait well.

Right now in the midst of this global pandemic, we're all waiting. Waiting for the stay-at-home orders to be lifted. Waiting for kids to go back to school. Waiting to go back to work. Waiting for the time when we're allowed to worship together again. Waiting for things to get back to normal. How do we wait well? What do we need to do so that our waiting doesn't lead to discouragement and despair? How can we wait in such a way without just escaping from the pain into distractions both benign and malignant?

Since what we're really waiting for as Christians is Jesus' return, let's look together at the last words in the Bible. There we'll see how a biblical view of waiting for our Messiah to return gives us the best way to wait well through any circumstance.

And he [an angel] said to me, "These words are trustworthy and true. And the Lord, the God of the spirits of the prophets, has sent his angel to show his servants what must soon take place."

"And behold, I am coming soon. Blessed is the one who keeps the words of the prophecy of this book."

I, John, am the one who heard and saw these things. And when I heard and saw them, I fell down to worship at the feet of the angel who showed them to me, but he said to me, "You must not do that! I am a fellow servant with you and your brothers the prophets, and with those who keep the words of this book. Worship God."

And he said to me, "Do not seal up the words of the prophecy of this book, for the time is near. Let the evildoer still do evil, and the filthy still be filthy, and the righteous still do right, and the holy still be holy."

"Behold, I am coming soon, bringing my recompense with me, to repay each one for what he has done. I am the Alpha and the Omega, the first and the last, the beginning and the end."

Blessed are those who wash their robes, so that they may have the right to the tree of life and that they may enter the city by the gates. Outside are the dogs and sorcerers and the sexually immoral and murderers and idolaters, and everyone who loves and practices falsehood.

"I, Jesus, have sent my angel to testify to you about these things for the churches. I am the root and the descendant of David, the bright morning star."

The Spirit and the Bride say, "Come." And let the one who hears say, "Come." And let the one who is thirsty come; let the one who desires take the water of life without price.

I warn everyone who hears the words of the prophecy of this book: if anyone adds to them, God will add to him the plagues described in this book, and if anyone takes away from the words of the book of this prophecy, God will take away his share in the tree of life and in the holy city, which are described in this book.

He who testifies to these things says, "Surely I am coming soon." Amen. Come, Lord Jesus!

The grace of the Lord Jesus be with all. Amen. (Rev. 22:6–21)

Soon and very soon. Doesn't seem soon enough does it? 2 Peter 3:8 tells us that with the Lord one day is as a thousand years and a thousand years is as one day. So I guess it's been two days since Jesus ascended into heaven?

Four times John writes "soon" in this passage, but we want soon to be right now. As Christians we often cry out, "Come Lord Jesus!" Sometimes it's out of a deep recognition of all that's broken in our lives, our community, and the world. More often than not it's because we don't like our current circumstances. "Come Lord Jesus" can be said in several different ways. We probably aren't thinking about Rev. 22:12 when we want Jesus to come soon: *"Behold, I am coming soon, bringing my recompense with me, to repay each one for what he has done."* I think the ESV translation team chose recompense over reward because what many will receive is no reward. Recompense communicates the idea of what's due. Jesus then tells us in Rev 22:14 that *"Blessed are those who wash their robes."*

Have you ever thrown a shirt out because you couldn't remove a stain no matter how many different stain removing products you try? Or maybe you have a favorite shirt that has a little stain on the side, and you keep hoping that this next time in the wash will take care of it. Perhaps you tell yourself it's just a little stain, and no one will notice, but every time you put it on and look in the mirror, it's the first thing you see. A little stain that won't go away.

We know that no effort on our part will remove the stain of our sins. We know that because we don't forget. Shame and guilt linger. We try again and again to do what's right and good but a thousand good deeds don't erase one sin. Even admitting our failure and asking for forgiveness doesn't take away the sin. It's done. It was done. It cannot be undone. So, when Jesus says, *"I am coming soon, bringing my recompense with me, to repay each one for what he has done,"* (Rev. 22:12) it should give us pause before we cry out "Come Lord Jesus".

Blessed are those who wash their robes? We can't. It doesn't make sense. No more sense that the idea of washing a white garment in blood.

> Then one of the elders addressed me, saying, "Who are these, clothed in white robes, and from where have they come?" I said to him, "Sir, you know." And he said to me, "These are the ones coming out of the great tribulation. They have washed their robes and made them white in the blood of the Lamb." (Rev. 7:13–14)

All our attempts to make sense of this fall into one of two categories. The first category is one of restriction—if you do this and don't do that, then you will keep your robes clean. The second category is one of license—you can do what you want, it doesn't really matter, and everyone's robes are dirty. Both fail to understand the work of Jesus on the cross and in our lives. It's addressed right here in this passage:

> *I warn everyone who hears the words of the prophecy of this book: if anyone adds to them, God will add to him the plagues described in this book, and if anyone takes away from the words of the book of this prophecy, God will take away his share in the tree of life and in the holy city, which are described in this book.* (Rev. 22:18–19)

We add to God's word all the time. We read the text as: "Those who are washed in the blood of the lamb are those who are upstanding and responsible members of society." Where does it say that? It's Jesus plus something. We know that when we add anything to Jesus, we get worse than nothing. We lose Jesus. The other side says, "Did God really say that we have to obey all these commands?" It's so easy to stray from one side to the other; we even do it on the same day. What's worse is that we encourage others to do the same. We are all guilty of encouraging others to add and take away from God's word. We're left again without any hope, save Jesus.

Our only hope is a righteousness that's not our own. A righteousness that's given to us through Jesus. That is why *"The Spirit and the Bride say, "Come"* (Rev. 22:17). The work of the Spirit is to point to Jesus, our only hope for redemption. The work of the Bride, the Church, is to point to Jesus our only hope for redemption. The Spirit of God and the Church cry out for Jesus to come back. And if we're going to wait well through any trial, we too must cry out for Jesus to come back and redeem.

At the end of *The Lord of the Rings* after helping Frodo complete his quest, Samwise Gamgee finds his friend the great wizard, whom he believed to be dead, and says,

"Gandalf! I thought you were dead! But then I thought I was dead myself. Is everything sad going to come untrue?"[1] Another big fan of *The Lord of the Rings*, Tim Keller, writes something similar, "Everything sad is going to come untrue, and it will somehow be greater for having once been broken and lost."[2] Jesus is the one who does this, the one who redeems, and it gives us hope for today as we cry out asking Him to do what he has promised to do.

Let's do this now. Let's cry out to Jesus asking him to redeem all that's broken right now in this world, in our country, our state, our city, our neighborhood, our family, our marriage, and especially our own hearts. Those who cry out to Jesus, asking him to redeem, are the ones who wait well for that redemption.

---

1. J.R.R. Tolkien, *Lord of the Rings: The Return of the King* (Boston, MA: Houghton Mifflin, 1995), 230.
2. Timothy Keller, *The Reason for God,* (New York, NY: Dutton, 2008), 33.

MEANDERING THROUGH MONOTONY

JED EDGAR

College in the Time of Corona

————

Jed is a student at Wheaton College in Wheaton, Illinois. He is working on a BS in Communications with a focus in Media Studies. He plays football, loves film, and wants to tell stories through screen writing and production. He is from Albuquerque, New Mexico.

————

An old, decrepit, slimy creature named Gollum lived deep in the cave near the murky waters. Gollum existed there alone, living for years on raw fish, wearing only a loincloth. Surrounded in his own filth, Gollum was content as his skin paled, teeth rotted, and livelihood worsened. His desires were pacified by an object of his greed. Gollum was happy in his miserable circumstances.

During Spring Break of 2020, my freshman year at Wheaton College was abruptly ended because of COVID-19. When I got the news that school was moving online, I was in bed in my childhood home, dreading the return to responsibilities. As I read the email from President Ryken, I was weirdly relieved. I still had to return to campus and gather my things, which I did with my dad and one of my sisters. We felt a little like Mad Max, entering a post-apocalyptic world on the run, shielding ourselves from catching this new virus. Even with that anxiety I still was glad to not have to return to the rigorous academic and athletic pressures of collegiate life.

Freshman year of college is already burdensome enough. I was uprooted from all forms of normalcy. I said goodbye to friends, family, and my home town. I had to adapt to a whole new reality and learn how to incorporate all the freedoms that independence brings.

While I was just beginning to flourish in this new reality, I had yet to reach the point of comfort. Just as I was getting to that point I became displaced in my displacement. I had to make the twenty-hour trek back to campus, pack up my belongings, and drive another twenty hours back. I felt like a tumbleweed rustling to and fro in the wind; settling for a moment before being uprooted again.

Still, I was cautiously optimistic. I would still have classes, but through a screen. Instead of my campus, I was surrounded by what I had grown up with—my posters, my bed, and my little brother barreling through my door.

This second half of my second semester felt like an extension of spring break, a part-time lead in to summer. And in many ways, it was.

I quickly sank back into the unhealthy habits of teenage male summer living. I stayed up into obscene hours of the night. I slept past noon when I didn't have a class—sometimes even if I did. I spent way too much time gaming, and I watched at least two movies per day all while living in an unkempt room of progressing filth. Ugh. Was I becoming Gollum?

My quarantine experience has been spent mostly dodging responsibility in favor of self-indulgence. I still met my requirements. I completed my assignments, I attended most virtual classes. I maintained my grades.

While I stayed on the Dean's List, I was content in my mediocrity. Quarantine living provided all I could desire, namely an excuse to live in semi-productive squalor without the consequences of a guilty conscience. I *was* becoming Gollum.

What I'm trying to say is my quarantine experience hasn't been filled with lament or restlessness but rather enjoyment, and that's perhaps the scariest thing about this weird phenomenon. I realize that as I say this, I'm healthy; knock on wood. The virus and the misery surrounding it has had little effect on me or my friends.

Initially, we had big quarantine plans. Austin was going to learn piano. Will planned to dip his toe in the waters of the culinary arts. Phil knew he'd become TikTok famous. Sasha had one book a week to read. My dad said he'd watch every Oscar Best Picture winner since 1960. And Wilson and I had a script to write.

There was a pressure to walk out of quarantine as a renaissance man, using this time as productively as possible. By week two we all came to the same epiphany—an abundance of free time doesn't mean you will produce anything. As the once bright flame of our spirit dwindled, so did our motivation.

But there's a problem. We live in a world that measures our worth in our productivity. This view of life is commoditized through things like YouTube, Instagram, music, and film. From a very young age, I was taught what the good life should look like through the media I consumed and I have found myself in a culture of comparison.

Little Johnny will watch a Logan Paul vlog on YouTube about living in the hills; Eric will listen to Drake sing about drugs, money and sex; Katy will see a post of Sommer Ray's body on Instagram, skewing her expectations of reality. We begin to compare our lives to theirs. In the process we become increasingly unhappy with the results.

If I feel content in the midst of this quarantine, it's

because I have been adrift for the majority of my life. Perhaps I'm like the title character in the Wes Anderson film *The Life Aquatic With Steve Zissou*. Renowned oceanographer Captain Steve Zissou is existentially lost during his final, melancholic sea quest for vengeance. Zissou cries out for purpose, meaning and understanding. He's adrift at sea and in his spirit. Zissou is able to fight himself out of this melancholic detachment by searching for something greater, something scarce—breathtaking beauty.

Zissou finds his beauty. Beauty in community. Beauty in family. Beauty in the transcendence of a Jaguar Shark.

I need beauty. Maybe that is what has been lacking the most in this quarantine. Beauty. Transcendence. I've been drowning in disembodied indwelling and comparison. I long for transcendence. I long for beauty.

I need beauty in the midst of a disruptive freshman year. I need it instead of what is offered to me through the screen. I need it like Zissou and Gollum. I need salvation from someone or something outside of me, because I know that I can't satisfy myself. My world offers me a well of pleasure and low-risk contentment to get me through the time of Corona. I return over and over hoping for more, yet every time I'm met with the same disappointment.

The water from the well of this cultural moment cannot fulfill me. As Dan Allen puts it, "Our hunger is infinite; it can never be satisfied with anything finite."[1]

The beauty in this world isn't meant to fulfill us. Only God can do that. And the great thing about God is that he is with me even in my discontentment. He is here. He is offering me grace and mercy for my failings. Exchanging my misplaced longings with himself. College quarantine life has brought me to the end of myself and to the beginning of the one who holds it all in his hand. I will rest in him, and trust that I will find contentment for my soul.

---

1. Mark D. Allen, et al, "The Ancient Saint Who Can Deal with Modern Doubts," The Gospel Coalition, Sept. 30, 2019, www. thegospelcoalition.org/reviews/road-saint-augustine-doubts-james-ka-smith/.

BALANCING THE PRODUCTIVITY SCALE

SARA JOY PROPPE

Work and Rest in the Time of Corona

———

Sara Joy Proppe is the founder and director of Proximity Project, an educational and consulting firm that equips churches to be creative stewards of their properties within the context of their neighborhoods in order to promote the common good. She is the co-host of the Embedded Church Podcast and writes and speaks nationally on the intersections of urban design, placemaking, and theology. She holds a BA in English Literature and a Masters in Community & Regional Planning.

———

A few years ago, I got meningitis. How I contracted it remains a mystery, but I ended up hospitalized for four days and on short-term disability from work for six weeks. To this day I have some strange side effects, including unexplained bouts of muscle aches and dyslexic typos in emails, neither of which showed up until post-meningitis life. Needless to say, it was a life-changing ordeal. I also carry with me another side effect, one which I consider a severe mercy bestowed upon me by God through that painful experience: the correcting of my pain scale.

The last morning I was in the hospital I was finally aware enough to take a shower and start packing my things to be discharged. I remember walking around my hospital room and seeing the pain scale chart on the wall —the one that has numbers ranging from one to ten with corresponding smiley and sad faces and descriptors below each number. What I saw shocked me. Based on this chart, I had been lying to the doctors about my level of pain for the past four days. Not purposefully lying; rather, I realized that my personal pain scale had desperately needed balancing. I had been telling my doctors that I was at a level five or six which conveyed moderate pain, yet I had been in significant pain. In my mind, however, I needed to have my entire arm ripped off before having any right to assert a nine or ten on the scale.

We all have different levels of tolerance, but this was more nuanced than simply having a high pain threshold. The pain scale revelation circled me back to words written about me in a letter of recommendation for an internship I had pursued many years earlier. My recommender had described me as one who is "faithful in her commitments, even to the point of pain." Though written to convey an honorable trait, the sentence gave me pause. Why do I sacrifice my well-being to make good on every commit-ment and not burden others? Why do I always feel the need to tough things out?

What I started to see is that much of my motivation was interwoven with fears. Fears of not achieving what I think others want, or being seen as weak and needy, or simply getting left behind. The flip side of this fear was the truth that I did not fully trust that Jesus loves me and that his work on the cross on my behalf is enough. Being authentic with my pain scale meant letting myself be at the mercy of my almighty God rather than what I think others expect. I am still plumbing the depth of this, but since meningitis I have learned that it is okay to reschedule things when I feel out of sorts, or to tell others when I am in pain, or to simply not be able to do it all. My limitations actually open up space to let Jesus carry me and my schedule. Discovering this has been a severe mercy.

This COVID-19 pandemic has brought my meningitis season back to mind often, particularly since that was a forced time of quiet and social withdrawal similar in many ways to the stay-at-home space I find myself in now. I have begun wrestling with balancing my productivity scale. Productivity is on high demand, perhaps partly as an attempt to emotionally avoid our current realities of loss and lament. It is easy right now to get immersed in the numerous articles on the best ways to be productive while working from home, or the top ten ways to quarantine with purpose, or the best methods for scheduling your days, and so on. To me it feels like a rat race to keep up with so much corresponding pressure to not let this time go to waste. However, the frenetic solutions and adaptations to this "new normal" will wane. In these coming weeks and months, levels of daily productivity will vacillate and likely dwindle. As many have noted, this is more like a marathon than a sprint.

While I believe God calls his workers to action, particularly in these times of crises, what if this crisis is a chance for us to balance our productivity scales in light of our relationship to God? If you are anything like me, you have erred on the end of seeking your value in what you do and what you produce. Can we learn to see that our work is valuable but not our value? Could we discover sweeter rest in Jesus and more space for thinking on that which is true, honorable, just, pure, lovely, commendable, and worthy of praise? I believe we will need to in order to embrace this severe mercy.

How do we adjust our productivity scales? I have not been productive enough to develop the ten-step solution for this, so I cannot offer you any panacea.

But I can encourage you with these words from the

Bible, words I will be holding onto tightly in this time. The simplicity and depth of Micah 6:8 helps me correct my productivity scale: *"He has told you, O man, what is good; and what does the Lord require of you but to do justice, and to love kindness, and to walk humbly with your God?"* (Mic. 6:8).

This life is not about boxes checked or to-do lists completed. It is about taking faithful steps in our callings alongside our savior. Jesus tells us, *"Consider the lilies of the field, how they grow: they neither toil nor spin, yet I tell you, even Solomon in all his glory was not arrayed like one of these"* (Matt. 6:28–29). During this spring season, sit with the beauty and intricacy of a flower and be reminded that God dresses the flowers of the field with no expectations for reciprocated productivity.

What a gift. Take heart. By the saving grace of Jesus, you are enough. Work heartily, as for the Lord and not for men.

A HISTORY OF FEELING

Poetry in the Time of Corona

———

The former US Poet Laureate Billy Collins has often referred to poetry as a "history of feeling." War and peace have their anthologies in every library to remind readers of the *actions* that accompany an age, but what about the feelings and impressions and emotions of an era? For that, we need poetry.

Poetry frames the impressions of human life into images for us to consider. But it also serves as a finger pointed to meaning; meaning that is often concealed in the most mundane nooks and crannies of life; meaning that often takes a little work and discipline to find. Perhaps these poems—written in the time of Corona—might offer just that: an invitation to find meaning in an age of unrest.

———

Baking Bread

Two cups of flour and half that of milk

along with a couple teaspoons of leavening
are all you need
to produce a loaf of soda bread to share
with butter and honey and flakes
of coarse sea salt after church in the garden.
A sturdy cutting board and one of those knives
with the long blade and jagged teeth
will help break the bread
into portions for hungry companions.
And that is all you need.

Joshua Burdette
Santa Barbara, California

————

Cluster

Every rejection replays in my blood vessels,
a flushed-cheek reminder that I am no island,
that my cloying need for you
—for anyone—
will stitch itself into my face
over and over
declaring itself, my failure, to the world.

Then again, maybe I am one.
An island, I mean.
Maybe I contain my own worlds,
twisting and buzzing and standing alone
through eras of change you will never know.
Maybe the lava flow of opt-in relationships
opting out again has brought me,
hiss by hiss,
closer to the sun.

Then again, maybe it is not a question
of self and strength but of society and good.

Because I can do it alone.
I can do it alone.
But who wants to do alone
what can be done together?

Maybe we don't escape the opting
one way
or another.
Maybe we are all islands.
But if I'm going to be an island,
I'd like to be part of an archipelago:
my own but not alone.

Susan Isaac
Santa Barbara, California

———

Familiarity in Isolation

Quiet Saturday mornings in quarantine:
fewer errands, yet more long-form essays
to read, to consume, to inform us of
the dangers and fears before us today.

Nothing seems normal in this new normal
except the laughter and wrestling
behind the door to the children's room,
the sounds of sipping coffee with
the distant whir of the pool pump's morning
laps around the too cold pool.

So much familiarity reframed in isolation,
wrapped in fear of the unknown.
This is the new normal that we pray
will soon give way to the next new normal
that includes more hospital beds to treat
all the normal hospital-required ailments of

the broken world that will remain until
Jesus returns to usher in
the one-day eternal normal with no tears, disease,
social quarantine, as we bask in
his glory in close proximity to each other
and with him in the eternal future normal.

Dan Smith
Tuscon, Arizona

———

Picnic on a Roof

From our picnic spot
Atop this hill of a mountain,
We see a house,

More mountains,
A curvy road,
And a car following its course.

We see puffy clouds,
And a hedgehog
On my water bottle.

We hear birds:
The peck of a woodpecker,
And the chickadee-dee-dee.

We feel happy
Because we hiked
To the top of this mountain.

And we are here—
Together, sharing this moment,
and some fruit snacks.

Willa Meinen (four years old) with her dad, John Meinen
Burlington, Vermont

———

Face Off

95% of COVID can be eliminated
By not touching your face
Slapping your face
Cursing your face
Seeing your face
Cutting your face
Hating your face
Comparing your face
To another face
Trying to save face
Hiding your face
Worshipping your face
Fixing your face
Covering your face
Cleaning your face
(Cutting off your nose
To spite your face?)
Running your face
Making a face
Poker face
Straight face
Her face
Clown face
Happy face
My face
Your face
Our face

What are we facing?
Please
Remember my face

Richie Sessions
Nashville, Tennessee

———

Honeysuckle

We
were on
that stretch of
road where it dips
down to kiss the creek
below and all our feet kept
walking but yours veered left
after your body was pulled by
your nose to the small patch
of honeysuckle and there
in the glow of sabbath
our city kids learned
to savor nature's
unexpected
gifts

Matthew Terrell
New York City, New York

———

The Crow

There in the garden sits a crow
perched on a palm branch.
He is searching
for scraps of bread and bits of carrot
tossed away by careless children and pressed
into the wet dirt beneath the table
back to the ground from which they came.

Children—like the birds—pay no attention
to sun or moon.
Their labor is measured in laughter and tears;
they are unaware of the effort required
to sow and thresh wheat
or the violent grind of the market
that produces food
in excess and casts
poor workers aside.

Here today and gone tomorrow
are the tears, the violence, the workers,
the wheat, and the children.
Yet a crow will remain in the garden.
Patient.
Vigilant.
Ready to peck the scraps from the earth and fly.

Joshua Burdette
Santa Barbara, California

———

Winston Salem, NC

I wore a mask today.
The string on the right side broke, next
To the onions. I didn't cry. No one was
Crying. Just shuffling between piles
Of produce and keeping distance.
How are you I asked the high schooler
Who weighed my produce and divided my food
into equal weights to not break the paper bag that
they no longer double up unless asked. And I
always forget to ask and then am too late.
I'm fine she said as her hands didn't touch the
bread. Didn't touch anything.
 That's how I loved her.

John Bourgeois
Wake Forest, North Carolina

———

Hiding from Non-malicious Torment

Steam rising
From the hour glass
of a favorite mug
warming my face, hands, and insides

Children
Interrupting my moment of quiet.
They're supposed to play
outside as I prepare for their school.
But I use the short moments
to soak in the quiet
like the lizard for which they hunt
soaks in the heat for the day.
I usher them back outside.

He is hiding
and I want to hide too
to stay undisturbed
for a few more minutes.
Sitting still now dreading
the return and request to
help them move
the sports equipment bin
to find the lizard in his nest.

Yes. Here it comes.
The door-squeak rushing open,
pleads to look up lizard traps
on the internet.
Negotiation and manipulation

attempted after the first "No."
Promises made by them
that will trap their souls
if followed through.
I refuse- wanting to encourage
creative problem solving
and preserve my brief moment
of silence in the day.
They leave. Grumbles continue to rise.

The lizard is spared
from non-malicious torment
even as my silent moment
ends for the day with my own
non-malicious torment
of children bored
with quarantine and homeschooling.

Dan Smith
Tucson, Arizona

———

Corona Easter

Sweatpant sitting
Firepit staring
Waiting for the world
To come back
 So much uselessness
A day can last a week
Screens burn my eyes
Helen and I fight
 And yet.
Birds lend their voices
To stories still unfolding
New life is forming

Lent and Spring

Scott Morris
Norman, Oklahoma

———

Sleep

Wriggling, arched
Grunting, deep breath,
Fighting the dark, she
Sings a song
To keep herself from
Stillness.

Toes forward, chest
Out and in and
Turning, she
Makes a noise,
Anything, to keep herself
From stillness.

My daughter fights sleep, like
I fight this long wait.

George Hamm
Louisville, Kentucky

———

On the Death of a Family Dog

I haven't checked but I'm sure
his coarse, brown hair is still
between the couch cushions.
His faded, red collar now sits
on the window sill above the

kitchen sink reminding me that
he was every time I wash my hands.

We looked through some old photos
and he was always there underfoot.
During birthday parties, Christmas
mornings, and quiet Sunday afternoons.
How many days did I not really notice
his presence? How many days will
I continue to notice his absence?

In the beginning he was like a furry son,
so small and needy. Then he became
my brother, a companion for long walks
on Saturday mornings and my
ever-present guardian as I worked at
the desk in the basement. At some
point he became my father, my elder,
showing me how to grow old and die
with some measure of grace.

When we brought him home on that
cold January night all those years ago
we had no idea.

Gavin Breeden
Cookeville, Tennessee

LOVE IN THE TIME OF CORONA

WHEN HOME IS NOT A SHELTER
JOSHUA BURDETTE

Parenting in the Time of Corona

————

*Joshua Burdette is the Pastor of Spiritual Formation and Coun-
seling at Christ Presbyterian Church in Santa Barbara, California. He earned a BA from Anderson University and an MDiv from
Covenant Theological Seminary. He is married to Katie, and they
have three children.*

————

I am both a pastor and a father. As a pastor, I take
Mondays off. As a father of three children under five-
years-old, however, Mondays begin like most other mornings—toasting waffles, spreading peanut butter, negoti-
ating the levels of milk in each cup, wiping faces, brewing
coffee, shushing screams, and attempting to regulate my
own rising anxiety. Yet in the time before Corona, those
children would be whisked away to preschool after break-
fast, leaving me with four glorious Monday hours of soli-
tude and autonomy each week. Not so anymore.

There is no preschool in the time of Corona; no child-
care at the gym; no date nights or baby-sitters. In short,

there are no breaks from the demands of domestic life apart from the demands of vocational life. And there is no rest for the weary.

We are *all* in grief over what we're experiencing, which means these small humans contain multitudes of feelings with few tools to process and interpret them. As we've seen our children erupt in tantrums, fighting, and erratic sleep, my wife and I have reminded each other again and again: *they are processing the loss of school and friends and play-dates in the only way they know how. Let's be gracious with them and try to prioritize connection over order.*

This past Monday off, I saw that my four-year-old son Jasper was spiraling out of control. I couldn't remember the last day he took a nap. Maybe a daddy-date and some special attention would help regulate his emotions and need for connection. I offered and his little face lit up. "Ice cream!" he exclaimed. I was feeling generous. I could detect the anticipation doing some good in my own heart as well. It was settled.

We braved the risk of the grocery store with masks and frequent squirts of hand sanitizer to get a box of popsicles—the kind made with real strawberries like a Mexican *paleta* and dipped in chocolate. We drove to the rose garden maintained by the historic Franciscan mission in our neighborhood. "I haven't been here in years!" Jasper exclaimed. It sure felt that way.

It was the perfect spot because it had plenty of space to keep distance and, since it was owned by the church, it was still open amid the park closures. We sat on an old stone wall at the bottom of a hill as Jasper devoured his popsicle. I looked at his face, covered in chocolate and focused intently on his task, and felt so much affection for him and gratitude for the peaceful moment. When he was done eating we played tag in the garden with vigorous laughter. Jasper got in the grass and rolled down the hill like a fish returning to water. It was absolutely beautiful. *This was a great idea. This was exactly what he needed. This was exactly what I needed. I bet everything will be so much easier now.*

Flash forward thirty minutes. We are back at home, and the moment is gone. I am wrestling to hold Jasper's writhing body on the living room rug as he kicks, bites, yells, and screams at the top of his little, but forceful, lungs, "I HATE YOU! LET ME GO!" I struggle to protect myself and his siblings.

Anxiety, adrenaline, and anger are pumping through my veins. My mind races. *What is wrong? What do I do? What happened to our beautiful moment? What do the neighbors think? Can Presbyterians do exorcisms?*

All of a sudden, his face turns tomato red, and he begins to quiver. Tears streak down the sides of his face. His gaze is fixated on a spot on the ceiling; his lips stretch sideways as a moan leaps out of his mouth. "OOOOOOHH. SPIIIDER! SPIIIDER! NOOOO!" he screams at the point above him. I look up, somewhat relieved that his rage is directed elsewhere. There's nothing there. No spider. Just white paint and a dusty light fixture.

God save me.

In the time before Corona we were barely hanging on. Now we are fighting for our lives every day. At night we shift to hostage negations as nightmares and fears of ninjas in one child threaten to waken the other two. We often play musical beds through the hours, wondering upon waking where and with whom we've slept. *Am I on the couch, in the kids' room, or my own bed?*

Unexplainably, our twelve-month-old, Felix, just began sleeping through the night and is currently the only one in the house getting a full night's sleep. Every day and every night are the same. The time of Corona is relentless.

When we hear people complain about the loneliness and isolation or the amount of movies they've watched, my wife and I bite our tongues. I'd kill for a day alone. We have no margins for movies. When the empty-nesters talk about their house projects; when the newlyweds talk about their board games and their deep conversations; when the productivity junkies talk about the things they've accomplished; when the contemplatives talk about their prayer walks—we grind our teeth.

We are in the trenches. We are surviving. We are prisoners of war. Listen, I know that we all bear our crosses and can't compare our stories. I am positively certain there are others suffering in far more tragic ways than me. But someone better pin a medal to my chest and pour me a glass of cold Moët & Chandon when this is over.

Don't worry. I know. That will never happen.

Perhaps that's one of the hardest parts of parenting in the time of Corona. In addition to the physical and emotional exertion, in addition to the loss of sleep and personal space, in addition to coming to the end of myself every single day, most of it goes largely unseen. No one sees how much I'm struggling to get by. In the time of Corona we are literally hidden behind the four walls of our house and a hedged-in yard. There are no breaks, and there are no "Job well dones." I don't understand how single and stay-at-home parents survive; they will forever have my unparalleled respect. For my part, this is the hardest thing I've ever done.

Maybe that's why in the midst of all this there is only one thing that has given my anxiety and exhaustion any comfort. It's not the assurance that it will get better someday. It's not the moments of pure joy and wonder that my children bring me on a daily basis. It's not even the hope that my best efforts are good enough to protect my children from lasting harm or that they will remember these days with fondness. Neither are likely.

The only thing that offers me any consolation is that God has revealed himself to be a God who sees. In fact, that's his first name, given by a vulnerable mother named Hagar by a spring in the desert wilderness: *"You are a God of seeing,"* she called him, adding, *"Truly here I have seen him who looks after me"* (Gen. 16:13).

He sees me too. He sees me trying to contain a little boy on a living room rug. He sees me sleeping on a twin bed surrounded by toys and costumes. He sees me cooking meals for children who refuse to eat them. He sees me playing tag in a rose garden. Perhaps he knows what it's like to father a strong-willed son full of intense fears, impulsive anger, and countless needs.

He sees my children too. He sees their little hearts and their big emotions. He sees their budding personalities. He sees their boo-boos and their lego towers. He sees their futures and the people they will become. He sees all our sins and his mercy that covers them.

If you are parenting in the time of Corona, take heart. He sees you too.

THE DAY OF SMALL THINGS

MIKE KHANDJIAN

Neighboring in the Time of Corona

———

Mike Khandjian is the Senior Pastor of Chapelgate Presbyterian Church, near Baltimore, Maryland. He attended Belhaven College and later earned his Master of Divinity from Reformed Theological Seminary. Mike has been married to Katherine for more than thirty-five years. Mike is the author of A Sometimes Stumbling Life: Making Sense of Our Struggles and God's Grace in the Journey of Faith.

———

"Little is large if God is in it."
—Leonard Sweet & Frank Viola
Jesus: A Theography

I was recently made aware of how a widow in our church phones her friend on Sunday morning. Her friend is also a widow, and she does not have internet service. They do this so they can worship together as our service streams— one on her computer and the other listening through her phone. Such a small, but beautiful expression.

A young woman in our church is a nurse on the front-line. She recently received a care package from a couple members of our congregation who quietly left it at her front door.

Small things.

Smallness and small beginnings comprise a theme that is woven throughout the Gospel's redemptive story. From the moment God created everything out of nothing, the big stories in the Scriptures demonstrate God's greatness with the obscure and unknown.

We can be glad for this. In spite of our own relative smallness, God invites us to collaborate with him in the daily course of his grand care of the world. It's not by shows of strength or displays of greatness. It's within the boundaries of our own limitations.

Zechariah prophesied that in time *"whoever despised the day of small things shall rejoice..."* (Zech. 4:10a). He foresaw the day when those who deemed the small things as meaningless would be given a new perspective. Have you considered that the small things you offer might be received as life-giving in big, unexpected ways?

My guess is that when all is said and done with this current crisis, we will look back and remember that to some extent we were sustained by the power of seemingly tiny gestures like a boy offering Jesus his lunch who in turn fed thousands with it.

It is the simple kindnesses, the meager offerings, the encouraging phone calls, the anonymous prayers, the neighborly acts, the invisible sacrifices—people caring for others in quiet ways that will likely not be detailed on the evening news—that will not be lost on the Father.

After all, isn't this what endears us to the Gospel? In God we have a Father who wrapped his Son in obscurity, in the smallness of a newborn—for the sake of his spectacular design for making us his? Isn't this our good news?

MOVING ON

SARAH VIGGIANO WRIGHT

Transitioning in the Time of Corona

———

Sarah Viggiano Wright is a teacher, speaker, and writer who loves sharing God's Word and equipping churches in their educational ministries. She is the author of A Living Hope: A Study of 1 Peter. *She contributed to* Co-Laborers, Co-Heirs: A Family Conversation *and* Beneath the Cross of Jesus: Lenten Reflections *and served as an instructor for the Teaching Women to Teach the Bible initiative through Reformed Theological Seminary. Sarah holds an MDiv and an MAC from Covenant Theological Seminary and serves Reformed University Fellowship (RUF) alongside her husband Lee and their three children.*

———

I am sitting in my partially decorated living room. This room was formerly filled with pictures and personal items, but now its walls are blank, and it mainly contains furniture. We boxed up our personal items to sell our home, and now our decor is packed in preparation of the move.

In January, my husband and I determined the Lord was

calling us to move to San Antonio, Texas. God brought us to Orlando from St. Louis to work with Reformed University Fellowship (RUF) at the University of Central Florida (UCF). For the past six years we have called Orlando home, but now we are transferring to take over the RUF at the University of Texas at San Antonio (UTSA).

This move was a decision my husband felt more strongly in favor of than I did. However I recognized this new position fit many of his gifts and desires, and we would be closer to family. So I am trusting God will provide friends and community as we take this next step. After all, leaving St. Louis was hard, but God provided such sweet friends, neighbors, activities, and memories for us in Orlando. I truly believe he will be faithful to us in San Antonio—he has always been faithful and he always will be.

But oh my goodness have I cried! January and February I cried and cried as I tallied our losses, realized our "lasts," listed all of our bucket list activities, and envisioned all the goodbyes we would have to make. To ease the sadness of all these partings, I knew we needed to do as many of our favorite things and see as many of our favorite people as we could particularly in March and April before we geared up in May for our departure.

Love Sought Is Good, But Given Unsought Better

Our first year in Orlando was challenging and isolating, but God ministered to our loneliness in such kind ways. Year-by-year God started layering the relationships that now make up our precious community.

We have been blessed with the best neighbors. They have taken us to Disney World, eaten holiday meals with us, and given gifts to our children "just because." Our neighborhood children have played with ours, and we've watched them grow.

We have loved and served Willow Creek Church. My husband Lee has preached and administered communion, and baptized two of our babies there. He's befriended men over lunch and golf. I've been able to lead worship, teach on Wednesday nights or at VBS, and attend our ladies' retreats. Moreover my friends (and Mom Squad) have been sources of inspiration, encouragement, laughter, and support as I have navigated wifehood, motherhood, work, and my walk with the Lord. Our children have loved the children's ministry, and Willow's preschool has been one of the biggest blessings to our family bar none.

Finally, we have been blessed with some incredible students and interns through RUF. It's been a privilege to get to know them, watch them grow, see them serve and discern the Lord's call on their lives, and move off to their next adventure after RUF. Compared to 2005 when I started in campus ministry as an RUF intern, I'm now significantly older, and I'm in a different life stage than our college students, so I feel justified in my maternal instincts to love, nurture, feed, guide, and protect them. They're my kids. I love them.

The mere thought of not seeing any of these precious people makes my heart ache, so in order to ease the blow of saying goodbye, Lee and I decided we would wait until after Spring Break in March. We also anticipated going to RUF's Summer Conference in early May where we would have time with our students and say our long goodbyes.

Something Foul's Afoot

In January, I had heard the first whisper of a really bad illness making its way to the American shores, but I thought it had been contained and was a non-issue. However as March began, I started hearing of the need to stay distant from people, wear face masks, and beware of dry coughs. I also discovered that it was incredibly difficult to find disinfectant wipes and toilet paper.

What was I missing? I had been preoccupied with publishing my book *A Living Hope: A Study of 1 Peter*, so there was quite a lot I had been saving to do for March and April. I started paying more attention to the news.

When Lee and I learned that this illness was particularly brutal on its victims' respiratory systems, it registered to us that our daughter who has these issues was going to be more vulnerable, and if she contracted it she would have extreme difficulty fighting it. A call to a doctor confirmed our suspicions, and our family decided to quarantine her. This was a hard decision at first because one of our dearest friends was getting married, and our whole family had roles in her wedding. But we decided my oldest and I would attend, and the rest of my family would stay contained. It was a drastic decision, and we worried if we were being paranoid—even though it was medically advised.

After my eldest and I returned, we started sheltering-in-place. However we naively hoped it would just be for a few weeks, and then things would go back to normal. After all, Spring Break was upon us, so really we wouldn't be seeing much of people anyway.

But Spring Break turned into an extended break and was followed by remote learning because of the COVID-19 pandemic. We began the adventures of educating our three children via distance learning, working from home, and ministering to our college students and our interns via phone calls, FaceTime, and Zoom group meetings.

A week into this venture, we were alerted that UCF's classes were all to be completed remotely for the remainder of the spring and summer semesters. All students living on campus housing were to return home immediately. The dorms would be closing down.

When Lee and I got the alert, our hearts sank. We wouldn't be able to reveal our departure in person. Our goodbyes would be virtual. We started adjusting our carefully thought out reveal-and-departure plan.

The week we decided to make our departure public, we started with our college students. Our Tuesday night meeting began the same way it always had (albeit on a

Zoom call): with songs, announcements, prayers, preaching, and more singing. But as the night was winding down, Lee and I sat in front of our computer screen beholding a gallery view of all of our college students. We took a deep breath and announced our departure.

The background chatter went silent, and we could see each student's expression of surprise and sadness.

With tears, we told them how much we loved them, how we felt the ministry was in a good place for us to transition, and how it was going to be passed on to a wonderful couple whom we trusted.

I could barely breathe—I had a huge lump in my throat, and it took a large amount of energy to keep from sobbing. This would have been the point where I would've wrapped my arms around each student, told them they could come to our house anytime to talk about it, and assured them that we could spend as much time together as possible before we moved. But I couldn't make any of those promises. Instead we all cried our tears quietly, staring at each other's faces, and surveying one another to see how everyone else was doing. It was miserable.

The call ended, and I cried more. Nothing felt right about it. This moment was never going to be easy, but now we were deprived of ways to comfort and console our students. They were already grieving their own losses and making their own adjustments. It felt like we were adding one more burden to the mix. It was hard, and there was nothing we could do to change it—which is par for the course in the time of Corona.

All throughout that week, we started making our phone calls to our sweet friends and community members. My heart ached each time I dialed a number to deliver the news, but God was kind in supplying us words of comfort and support through our friends.

At the next week's RUF Zoom meeting, we asked our students how they were doing. God was ministering to them to the point where they could provide expressions of "Congratulations" commingled with "Thank you" and "I'll miss you." I was blown away by how mature all of their responses were. They are such great students!

April was now over, and it looked as though our list of "last things" was going to be relatively unaccomplished. The last time I was going to lead worship became a recording broadcast on Facebook Live on Easter Sunday. The last time we were going to go to Disney World with our neighbors was now cancelled. The last trips to see our Florida friends outside of Orlando were cancelled. My Teaching Women to Teach the Bible class had been cancelled. This was not the exit I had envisioned at all. The once well-scripted closing to our Orlando Act was turning into a Shakespearean Tragedy.

While UCF had been decided for a month, the Orange County Public School district was holding out on their decision of whether to go back to school starting May 4. But toward the end of April, the school district decided to finish the rest of the school semester via distance-learning. Now we had to break it to our own children that they may not get to see their teachers or classmates in-person again. The little shred of hope for normalcy we were holding onto was now gone, and another cycle of grief began. Our three-year-old didn't seem to understand, but our seven and five-year-olds were brokenhearted.

We have all had significant emotional outbursts from the stresses of moving and sheltering-in-place, but there was a particularly poignant one that came from one of our children. We were getting geared up to go to a car parade with her classmates to celebrate her precious teacher (who is retiring), and she kept crying, "Mommy, I'm scared. I'm so scared."

In a moment of clarity that truly came from the Holy Spirit, I understood what she meant. She was scared of saying goodbye, scared of the pain inside her heart that loves so big, and scared of not knowing what was next. My mother's heart grieved *with* her and *for* her, "Me too, my love. Me too."

The cycles of grief have been recurring often the past several months. I know we are not alone. Everyone has had their life altered or affected in some way. The distress of the limitations of COVID-19 are felt by all, and some people are experiencing significantly more profound losses: loss of jobs, loss of loved ones, loss of health, and more. My family has been relatively spared the more profound losses, and for that I am grateful. But every time a friend is in the hospital and we can't visit, a loved one dies and we can't be there for the funeral, or a baby is born and we won't be able to meet him or her, we have the additional loss of wondering whether or not will be able to see that person anytime soon. The grief is real and the pain is felt.

There are multiple kinds of pain at hand—sad pain from grief and losses, and also the "good" pain that comes from loving people so deeply and from being loved so well, that the disconnection hurts. I am grateful that most of our pain has been "good pain."

I'm not making peace with pain—pain is not the way it supposed to be—but the reasons why it hurts are rooted in love. As William Shakespeare accurately penned in *Romeo and Juliet*, "Parting is such sweet sorrow."[1]

There have been some bright spots during these isolated times. We've participated in three parades celebrating teachers, and although we couldn't get out and hug our friends (another extreme exercise of restraint for extroverted Italians), it was a balm to behold them face to face. And for those whom we knew it was the last time to see them, we got to express how much they meant to us.

Another mercy has been our home selling process. We listed at the beginning of April thinking that the COVID-19 climate would bring a lot of financial instability, and thus we would have to wait a while for our home to sell. We also had to make modifications to the showing process by not having open houses and scheduling tours

—with masks and gloves—by appointment only. We were hoping to sell by June, but our fourth day on the market we were under contract and scheduled to close by the end of May. While the timing was earlier than we thought, to sell is a gift. Next we worried on *how* to pack everything ourselves with school, work, and three young kids in-tow. Yet another kindness of the Lord is the newfound ability to schedule services to help with our move, as some of the smaller businesses in Florida have recently reopened.

A final mercy is that now we may be able to do some sort of parade, and while I will not able to hug each person, it will at least be a goodbye.

Here I am in my living room, sitting on the couch that has hosted game nights, watch parties, happy catch-ups, and students whose lives were falling apart. The room has hosted small group Bible studies, seminars, girls and guys nights, reveal parties for where our students would do their own RUF internships, and even the gender reveal when we learn our third child would be our son.

Here I am firmly in the grip of my Savior, the One who has conquered sin, death, hell, and COVID-19. He is the One who comforts me as I cry for the losses and the things I cannot change. He is the One who gives me hope in the reminder that all suffering is momentary compared to the glory that lies ahead (2 Cor. 4:17; 1 Pet. 1:6). He is the One holding the loved ones I didn't get to bury as well as those who mourn them, the babies I didn't get to hold, and the friends I didn't get to hug goodbye. In all this he is good all the time. He is on his heavenly throne ruling over all things and working them out for his glory and my good, even in the time of Corona.

---

1. Shakespeare, William, 1564–1616. Romeo And Juliet, 1597. (Oxford: published for the Malone Society by Oxford University Press, 2000), Act II, Scene ii.

BAKING BREAD AND MAKING LOVE

JUSTIN EDGAR

Domestic Life in the Time of Corona

———

Justin is the Senior Pastor of City Presbyterian Church in Albuquerque, New Mexico. He holds a BS in Secondary Education from New Mexico State University and an MDiv from Westminster Theological Seminary. Prior to serving in New Mexico, Justin worked in churches in Albuquerque, Lubbock, and Rockwall. Justin is married to Danette, and they have three sons and two daughters.

———

My wife shared the following meme with me: **Apparently when you take sports away from men you get sourdough bread, and I'll be honest, I did not see that coming.**

Based on the missing ingredients in most grocery stores, I think this is true. During the last nine weeks, the aisles featuring flour and yeast have been sparse. Every time I tried to order online or for grocery pick-up, these items were shaded with the words "out of stock" next to them. So for every grocery run, I would hunt the aisles and take whatever flour I could find. My wife had her parents share their Vitamix, and my father-in-law would grab a bag of whole wheat grain, which he hauls for a living so we could make our own flour. Corona has made bakers of us all.

For me, it started when one of my congregants shared pictures of the bread her husband made on Facebook. They were baking bread, eating bread, and giving bread away. I thought maybe I should be baking bread, eating bread, and giving bread away, though that would be a new thing for me. My wife and I did own a bread maker long ago, early in our marriage.

But this was different. The bread my friend made was sourdough. Her bread was artisan. It was crusty and beautiful not soft and delicate. It would be new, because over the last ten years or so I haven't really been a bread guy. Now I love sourdough bread, and on occasion would buy a loaf from the store.

I had determined bread was bad because of my continual battles on the scale. I didn't want the grain gut, even though I had it. I regularly danced between keto and Adkins diets—no bread. I didn't buy and certainly didn't make it.

But over the course of the last two years, the scale battle was swayed through the wonder of weight-loss surgery. This has diminished some of my fear of grain. I am not suddenly carb loading, but I do enjoy some carbs now and again. Bread was once again an option.

Then Paul Hollywood came into my life. Paul Hollywood is the one consistent celebrity chef on the *Great British Baking Show*. I am a fan of the show and have a bit of a man-crush on Paul. Paul is part Simon Cowell and part a British Guy Fieri. He's cool. He's a little harsh, and he can bake. Bread is his specialty. Hollywood knows his bread.

Since domestic life was now my life, I was unencumbered by much of my regular work routines, and full-up with free time due to COVID-19. I now had the time to bake. I asked my friend for some starter.

Starter is the secret sauce of sourdough bread. I still don't know how to *start* starter at least from the ground up. But my friend does, and she was willing to share, so she came over and grabbed a Mason Jar. She dropped off a loaf that she and her husband had made and told me she'd leave the jar at the door in a few days, and I would have my starter.

By the week's end, I had my first bread baby. A bread baby is starter that must be regularly fed. This feeding helps the yeast to remain active and helps it to grow. To further care for this bread baby, she shared a series of videos that her husband made which guided me through the feeding, making, and baking process.

For this I needed flour, which I had at first, because we always had flour in our home. We just rarely used that flour. But we had it. I also needed water, salt, and a couple of cast iron pans or dutch ovens. These I also had.

I watched the videos. I watched them again and again. As I began to make and then bake, I watched them again. On bread days my wife and one of my daughters could guide me through the process from the couch, because they heard the videos so many times playing from my phone in the kitchen.

I would feed the baby, which was added to 950 grams of flour and 500 grams of water and then 20 grams of salt. I would form, flatten, and fold the ingredients together, and then fold them again and again and again.

Then I would let the bread prove. At first, the proving happened in my oven in the pans with some hot water creating the right temperature and environment for the dough to rise. A few days after my first bake, I ordered proving baskets on Amazon to make it easier and better.

What matters most in all of this at least for the finished product is the rise. That's why you need the starter. The yeasty bread baby does the work. That yeast is a living being, a bacteria that gives the bread its rise and its sour, tangy flavor. As the bread is folded and proved it metabolizes the starches and sugars in the flour, turning them into alcohol and carbon dioxide. This gas inflates a network of air bubbles which causes the bread to rise. As long as the starter is active and the environment is correct, the yeast will do its job. But bread making is all about the rise. Folding and proving, air and temperature, coupled with active ingredients gives you the rise. With bread baking there is immediate feedback—did it rise, or is it flat?

My first *boule* miraculously did rise. As did my second and my third. But they didn't ever seem to rise quite enough. I remember hearing Paul Hollywood's English voice, "That bread is under-proved. That one is over-proved." The *ou* of his "proved" echoed in my ear. I wasn't sure what over or under even meant, but I was certain my bread was one or the other. Either my bread split internally, stretched too much, or it was thick, heavy —"stodgy" as Hollywood might say.

I was still proud of it. My friend's recipe had me adding rosemary, and that adds this wonderful scent and flavor to the bread. Toast became a regular morning staple after coffee. The bread crisp on the edges, with this rough crust and silky in the middle. With lots of butter and a hint of salt, it is so, so good. I shared it with my one of my daughters and two of my sons. They loved it.

The rest of the fam doesn't do gluten or they don't do sourdough, and that was truly their loss. Each time I would bake, I would bake two loaves. And I would bake every two or three days. This meant too much bread for the four of us that ate it. Then I began giving the bread away. It became a nice way to bless others while sheltering in place.

Baking bread became a way not only to love my immediate family but others. As I gave the *boules,* I would hear back how much others loved the bread. I was becoming a baker. I wondered if Hollywood would be proud? Probably not. My rise was still inconsistent, and it never really hit the Hollywood high peaks.

The bread bakers also increased on my social media feed. Was this due to the influx of bakers due to quarantine or due to the algorithms of Instagram or both? Either way, I quickly found myself comparing my *boule* to the ones on my feed. Why are theirs so pretty? Why is their peak so high? How do I make it look like that? My bread-righteousness was now wounded, and it soon took another hit when about halfway through the quarantine, I baked two flat and stodgy loaves.

They were so ugly. So flat. So heavy. There'd be no sharing of these on the gram or anywhere else. Over the next few days I was surly. Everything my family did bugged me. I was irritated and irritable. I was sour.

What had set me off? Was it really flat bread? Really? During these few days, I also scoured the internet. I diverted from the videos from my friend and ventured out to other lovers, I mean recipes. One suggested adding some dry yeast to my starter and flour. Another said to buy diastatic malt powder. I watched more YouTube clips. I bought smaller cast iron pans so my peaks might rise, and I started decorating the tops of the *boule* with a razor blade. And my bread rose again. And I found myself happy again. My Instagram posts filled with likes and comments. A baker friend who started a macaron company was telling me how pretty my *boules* were. Happy again, I shared my loaves with others.

What started out as a way to distract myself, turned into a way to love others, which turned into a way to feel okay. What happened?

My heart happened. Theologian John Calvin says our hearts are idol-making factories. We can turn anything into an idol, even sourdough. My bread was my right-eousness. The rise and Hollywood's voice was the law. Bread day was transformed from a way to enjoy something in the midst of Corona and shelter in place, from a way to love others, into a way to be enough.

All of domestic life finds itself here, whether it's a meal, or a clean house, or well-behaved children, or devotions around a table, or broken things easily repaired, or making love with your spouse. Domestic life curves in.

Martin Luther called this *incurvates in se*. We are so curved in upon ourselves that we use both physical and spiritual goods for our own purposes and in all things we seek only ourselves.[1] Dave Zahl adds the following: "What Luther means is that despite our best efforts to love and serve others to the best of our ability, human beings find it impossible to escape the gravity of self-interest, and we are often unconscious of this fact, even as it drives our behavior."[2] Domestic life can be a great gift, a way to share the love of God with family and friends. It can be a way to make room for others. But it can also be a way to love yourself, to garner praise, to be enough in your eyes or the eyes of your family, your neighbor, or your church. I started this wanting to love my family by sharing with them the flavor and beauty of sourdough, but I found myself frustrated and angry if my bread didn't rise.

Bread is really a food of life and love. Leon Kass writes, "Man becomes most human with the eating of bread."[3] Norman Wirzba adds, "To get bread, people must transform grain into flour, change flour into dough, and then bake it at the right temperature for the right time to get something worth eating."[4] Jesus used bread as a reference to the kind of life he offers. It is a full life. A life of sustenance. A life of love. He invites us to ask for our daily bread, so both our tummies and tables might be full. Bread is the stuff of domestic life. It is a way to love.

Bread and all food is also a way to remember death. Wirzba highlights this in his book *Food and Faith*. When we make bread, we need death. Something has to die for us to live. Wirzba writes, "Death decays into each loaf and reemerges as new life. All because of the astounding complex and mostly invisible work of billions of bacteria and microorganisms."[5] The soil, the grain, and the starter provide the hospitable stuff where life grows.[6] Wirzba quotes Wendell Berry as Berry describes soil in Christ-like terms:

> The most exemplary nature is that of the topsoil. It is very Christ-like in its passivity and beneficence, and in the penetrating energy that issues out of its peaceableness. It increases by experience, by the passage of seasons over it, growth rising out of it and returning to it, not by ambition or aggressiveness. It is enriched by all things that die and enter into it. It keeps the past, not as history or as memory, but as richness, new possibility. Its fertility is always building up out of death into promise. Death is the bridge or the tunnel by which its past enters its future.[7]

Domestic life happens with this death bridge constantly in view. Life comes from death. Domestic life is the common life where sacrificial love is enacted and lived out. We die to ourselves so our family, our neighbors, our guests might live. The very food we serve is meant to remind of this. The love of God is scored into the very dough of domestic life.

This is the beauty of food. It is never just earthy. It is ripe and full of life, and that life always comes through death. The Gospel written in every *boule*. My curved-in and idol-making heart makes an idol of even bread. It needs this type of love.

My family does too. Each *boule* I made for them was intended to be a domestic act of love during a time when death seemed most especially close. But death is always close around a table. Early on with my children, Wirzba's insights about food and faith were taught and ingested. My daughter would pray for every meal in this way. "Thank you God for this food. Thank you for the farmer who planted the grain so that we could make the bread, thank you for the ranchers who fed the cows, the cows that gave their life, so that we might live. Thank you for the butcher who cut the meat, for the truck driver who delivered the food to the store, the store that sold the food, and thank you for my mom and dad who made it."

There was this connection that she made to the sacrificial love of domestic life. A golden line of life and love. Jesus is always offering himself to us, and each *boule* and meal is a way that not only he offers himself to us, but that we offer ourselves to others. Corona has provided us with a rich context to remember death and life once again around a table set and a loaf prepared. This is my body broken for you, take and eat and live. Curve yourself around Christ. His death for your death. His life for your life.

Domestic life is always a life of love and sacrifice.

---

1. Martin Luther, Luther's Works, vol. 25, p. 345, see also pp. 291-92
2. Dave Zahl, "Incurvatus in Se." *Mockingbird*, 13 Oct. 2015, mbird.com/glossary/incurvatus-in-se/.
3. Norman Wirzba, *Food and Faith* (p. 13). Cambridge University Press. Kindle Edition.
4. Ibid. p. 13.
5. Ibid. p. 13.
6. Ibid. p. 14.
7. Ibid. p. 14.

WE'RE ALL IN THIS TOGETHER...
UNTIL WE AREN'T

SUSAN ISAAC

Human Nature in the Time of Corona

———

Susan has spent the last decade working with teenagers, first as a high school English teacher and now as the Assistant Principal and Director of Spiritual Life at Providence School in Santa Barbara, California. She has a BA from California State University, Northridge and an MA from Pepperdine University.

———

Have you ever read *Lord of the Flies*—William Goulding's delightful but dark 1954 novel about a group of boys who get stranded on a desert island? They start off thinking it'll be a jolly good time but end up turning savage and killing each other. Yeah. We're all living that.

Whenever a crisis starts, there is an outpouring of community love and support. People put signs in their yards and windows declaring, "We're All in This Together," or "Stay Home and Stay Safe." We see news stories of good Samaritans donating food to the frontline healthcare workers. We watch the young care for the elderly.

And that's all good and well—for a month or so. But

what happens when that month becomes two months? Three months? A year? What happens when the bloom is off the community rose? *Lord of the Flies*. That's what.

I live in a beautiful part of downtown Santa Barbara. I'm one of the lucky jerks who has access to beautiful walks through neighborhoods of Spanish- and Craftsman-style houses. One such walk is the route between my house and the Mission Santa Barbara—a charming destination with a historic chapel and a community rose garden. Since moving to Santa Barbara three years ago, this walk has become one of my favorites. It has enough of a hill to be a justifiable workout, plenty of interesting homes and yards to look at, and few pedestrians to distract me from my podcasts.

Before COVID-19 drove us all into social distancing, I would take this walk about once a week. Now that I work from home and stare at my computer what feels like 135 percent of the time, I take this walk almost daily.

When the stay-at-home order began back in March, these walks were mostly pleasant. I would bemoan the crowded paths as every person in my neighborhood also increased their walking quotas, but I loved that people were greeting me as we passed. Granted, I suspect this was to counterbalance the fact that we were all crossing the street or stepping into the road whenever we saw each other, because two months ago everyone was taking the six-foot rule very seriously. Still, it was nice to feel so neighborly.

Some of us wore masks, some didn't, but we all made it work. I would walk past houses with signs in their windows or on their lawns and think, *Heck yeah—we are all in this together!* One house consistently had—and still has as I write this—a rotating melange of encouraging chalk messages written in bright colors and festive fonts on their sidewalk, swapping out uplifting platitudes every few days, but always using at least four joyous exclamation points!

But as March wore on to become April, and April

droned into May, I began to notice something. People weren't quite as willing to step into the road and maneuver around parked cars to give each other space. People with masks were shooting judgmental eye lasers at those without (I know this because I fall into the latter category—go ahead and shoot your distance judgement lasers). People stopped greeting me and returned to the pre-Corona method of looking down at the concrete or pretending that their phone had suddenly pinged for their attention. And this backslide wasn't just in my neighborhood; I began to notice it everywhere.

Customers were ignoring the blue X's meant to keep us six feet apart in stores and take-out lines. Drivers were honking more and driving more aggressively despite the still-not-as-crowded-as-normal-roads. Maskless customers were getting angry at Trader Joe's employees for both enforcing the mask rule and not providing the general public with masks. Customers behind the maskless ones grew even more frustrated that these yahoos thought they could break the rule while the rest of us drowned in our own chin sweat while we stood under the 87-degree spring sun.

As this public angst became more prevalent, it hit me —the bloom is off the Corona rose.

This truth crystalized in my mind on Tuesday of this week when I went on my beloved (if not redundant) walking route to the mission. It was a warmish afternoon, the type that would melt a non-native Californian but wouldn't really impress an Arizonan. While walking uphill and starting to build up a justifiable workout sweat, I looked up to "F*** YOU" written in pleasant pastel orange chalk on the wall of one of the houses. This was a surprise because 1) I don't think I've ever really thought of orange—pastel or otherwise—as an aesthetically pleasing color, but for whatever reason this particular shade really worked with the stone on which it was written and 2) well, someone was telling me and everyone else to f*** off. Up until to this point, all of the chalk messages I had seen around town were uplifting reminders to be kind to one another and that we were loved. This was a sharp left turn into negative chalk talk for which I was unprepared.

Our Western world likes to think that if we just try a little tenderness, we can work our way through anything. We believe a sense of community and our plucky United-Statesian can-do spirit will pull us through the hard times. But that isn't the case. Just go on social media and you will see that we are back at our pre-Corona antics. We're calling each other idiots or sheep or communists, defending our right to post conflicting and poorly researched articles while vilifying others of doing the same, and ripping each other apart over disagreements. We've gone right back to our old divisiveness, to a mindset replete with figurative "f*** you" chalk messages. And it only took a matter of weeks.

Perhaps if you're honest, you see this in your own heart as well. As I sit writing this, it is 7:12am, and I am trying my level best not to lose my temper as my neighbors let their young son play with their leaf blower. Granted, I can imagine how rough it is to have a toddler at home all day every day for this long. I can also imagine how fun it may be to use a high-powered leaf blower to send your toy cars scuttling down the street. But what I can't imagine is how the adults in this situation think this is acceptable at 7 in the morning. Each time that leaf blower starts and stops and starts again, my blood boils just that one degree more at the inconsideration of it all, not to mention the extremely grating sound of the crow who has decided to nest in the tree in front of my house. I'm don't think I'm about to write a chalk expletive on their fence, but I am considering writing a strongly worded letter and throwing something (to the family and at the crow, respectively).

A lot of our bootstraps are close to snapping, if they haven't already. We want to go to our friends' homes. We want to go to the beach. We want to sit down in our favorite restaurants. We want to fill our sanctuaries on Sunday morning and have a tangible reminder of the body and blood of Christ. We want our children to be quiet for, just maybe, five consecutive minutes. We want so many things that are not really options right now, and that frustrated desire is revealing the true depth of our nature more than we may like to admit. That frustrated desire is giving us an all too close look into our primal, animalistic natures, our innate defensiveness, and our get-off-my-lawn anger.

This unmasking (too soon?) of our true natures is terrifying—just ask Piggy from *Lord of the Flies*. But it is ultimately necessary in order for us to stop buying into the lie that if we just work harder, everything will be okay. As Americans, we like to believe that we are naturally equipped with the right stuff—whatever that stuff may be —and that we can make it out of any crisis because we're great. The reality is we may feel that way because of our relative wealth, comfort, and freedom. We've been floating down the river of life, feeling confident as we pass through life's swirling eddies, until we get to the actual rapids and realize that we've been riding a flimsy inflatable swan the whole time. Yeah, we've been sitting pretty comfy up on our cushy bird throne, but that glorified balloon isn't about to protect us from anything. But if we don't realize the foolishness of the swan, we may never stop putting our hope in it.

Even as Christians we often put our hope in relationships, family, possessions, or even government before we put our hope in God. And the nefariousness of this is the sneaky, subconscious nature of it all. Over and over again in Scripture we see God using crises to bring his people back to him—famine, plague, desert wanderings (which will probably be recreated by Instagram influencers now that Coachella has been canceled).

Maybe we needed this pandemic to go on this long to realize how little of our lives and our tempers we can actually control. As we come to the end of our own efforts, we see how desperately we need a savior—a savior that will ultimately provide much more than a vaccine or an economic stimulus plan or a short-cut back to being "normal." If ever there were times when I knew I needed Jesus, it's been in the darkest moments of my life, when death and uncertainty loomed heavy over my spirit. It's been those moments when my metaphorical swan finally deflates and reveals itself to be the cheap plastic air-filled sack that it is.

The Lord of the Flies ends in a quick deflation into neediness (spoiler alert!). The boys are saved by adults, the very adults they were at first happy to be free from. And what do they do when they are rescued? They weep. All of them. They collapse back into their childish neediness, crying their little hearts out as they, for the first time in months, feel a sense of release. And what makes them finally feel that release from the burdens they've carried? The presence of someone else, someone bigger than them who can actually protect them and save them from each other and their own dark hearts.

We have that in Jesus. We have a savior much bigger and stronger and more able than us, whose very presence makes all of our efforts to save ourselves seem childish and useless, but whose arms are nonetheless open to receive our weak, weeping, arrogant selves. And praise the Lord for it because I could really use a hug right about now.

DISTANCE LEARNING
ALEX BOSGRAF

Campus Ministry in the Time of Corona

———

Alex has served as Campus Staff for Reformed University Fellowship (RUF) at Boise State University in Boise, Idaho, since 2014. Alex graduated from the University of Georgia and is pursuing a Masters of Arts in Counseling at Westminster Theological Seminary.

———

By the first week of March 2020, most of my conversations with students centered on the coronavirus. They asked me what it was, what I thought about it, and if I was nervous. We talked over coffee about their Spring Break plans and how they might be affected if things got worse. At our weekly lunch in the Student Union Building, they told stories of friends from schools like Notre Dame and Stanford who were being sent home or told not to return to campus after break.

On March 13, after a day full of conversations about what might happen, Boise State announced that they would be moving all classes to an online platform and asked students to move home for the rest of the semester. In the span of an hour, everything changed

I spent the next week texting and calling students to touch base about decisions they were making and how they were holding up. Their responses ranged across the spectrum, which didn't surprise me. A few were excited to do school from home. The thought of avoiding the crowds of lecture halls and getting to stay in the comfort of home sounded great to them, even exciting.

But for the majority, reality set in quickly. How would they stay on top of classes while packing up their whole life in under a week? Would they cancel their flight home for Spring Break and instead have their parents drive sixteen hours to Boise, empty their dorm room, and drive sixteen hours back? Was this the last time they would see some of their closest friends and classmates in person? Would they have a graduation?

Freshmen and new students were just getting settled into college life. They were starting to connect with people, plug in with clubs, and find on-campus jobs and volunteer opportunities. Freshmen weren't even away from home for a year before they were sent back.

For the seniors, the impact was devastating. Most of them had worked so hard to get to this point to celebrate their accomplishments with parties, events, and a major ceremony to mark the end of college and the commencement of their professional life. All of the "lasts" they had been looking forward to—counting on—would no longer be possible.

On top of the jarring end to their college experience, their entrance into the job world would be even harder than they had anticipated. Companies and schools that might have considered hiring a new graduate prior to the pandemic were hit hard economically and forced to let veteran workers with years of experience go. Why would they hire these inexperienced graduates?

In the midst of all of this upheaval, anxiety, and uncertainty, what can a campus ministry do? The RUF staff asked ourselves this question as we sought to maintain connection with each of our students. We thought our presence in their lives—even from a distance—could be helpful and supportive, so we adjusted as much as possible. We do ministry at three levels: large group meetings, small groups, and one-on-ones. Thanks to technology, we were able to continue doing each of these.

Boise State's RUF participated in a Zoom large group meeting that included schools all over the Western US. Student leaders hosted and led Zoom small groups, and staff hosted a weekly "How to Study the Bible" seminar, game night, and prayer time. One-on-ones continued over the phone, FaceTime, and Zoom, as long as students were not too burned out from being on screens that day.

Those one-on-one "meetings" filled the bulk of my time for the last six weeks of the semester. So many of our female students wanted to talk that I had to limit how many conversations I could set up each day. The loss of in-person relationship was taking a toll, but we were glad to have some way to connect. I spent hours of conversation time with students who were struggling to process their feelings and reactions to the adjustments they had to make.

There were too many conversations to have, and I began to see the reality of my own limitations. I deeply wanted to care for every student possible but I was coming to the end of my capacity. I was reminded over and over that as much as I loved my students, God loved them even more. I would have to entrust them to his care and engage their faith through listening.

I asked questions like, "How did you feel leaving campus? What are you sad about missing? What is it like being home (or alone if they didn't go home)? How is online school going? What do you do in your free time? How is your family? What are some ways I can be praying for you?"

It was heavy to walk through each of their experiences, and I was exhausted. My pastor helped me realize that everything was new in my life as well. Not only were we unable to be physically present to support students as we normally would, but we were also walking every single one of our students through the same thing. Typically, we have students facing different experiences at different times. There will be a handful of students who are deeply struggling and need intensely focused care. A few students will have news to share and process through. Some students might have questions about Christianity.

This season was a time of walking each student through their personal responses and emotions to a shared crisis, one that was changing my own life as well. My roommates and I needed to cancel a trip to Italy we had been planning for a year. I had to work from home and learn to do ministry virtually. I was facing my own sadness and disappointments. Realizing how deeply this was affecting all of us helped me have more grace with myself and see my profound need to trust in and commune with Jesus.

It is painful to sit on the other end of the phone while someone cries and not be able to comfort them with a touch to their hand, an encouraging nod, or tears in your own eyes. Listening just sounds like silence.

A student who had just started re-engaging her faith with our community cried with me out of fear and frustration. Would she be able to stay connected to people she had just met? Why would God pull her out of community and into the isolation she was already so afraid of falling back into?

Another woman, a graduating senior, couldn't hold back tears as she talked through all of the things she would miss out on during her last semester of college. She mourned the loss of graduation and the events she was looking forward to and shared her stress about planning a wedding during a time full of unknowns. My sister, also a senior finishing college, tearfully told me she knew it was okay to be sad, but she was just really tired of being sad.

Campus life and ministry is so relational, so centered on physical presence. I have felt the loss of this presence deeply. But God has provided ways for us to continue to talk and walk together through a confusing time. Praise the Lord that these women are willing to be honest over the phone, to face what they are feeling, and to express it to someone who cares. Because of the Gospel, we can celebrate God's grace as well as grieve with our students.

What has been comforting and motivating for me during this time is that God is at work. A colleague reminded me that God was at work on the worst day—the day of Jesus' crucifixion—to bring about his plan of redemption. He is working out his plan of redemption on this hard day, too. When things look out of control, we can be sure that God is still bringing salvation to the ends of the earth.

I would not choose to scatter my students from Idaho all the way to California, Wisconsin, and Alaska. That doesn't seem like the best way to reach and equip them with the Gospel. But I trust that God will use it. His plans are far greater than I can know or imagine, and that helps me pursue these students and encourage them. If he can use the brutal crucifixion of his beloved son to bring near those who are far off, he can use the effects of this virus as well.

Even if wedding and travel plans get changed? Even if students can't move to campus in the fall? Even if I feel exhausted? Even if depression and anxiety start showing up more than ever before? Even if we are making it up as we go? Yes, even then.

LOSING MY RELIGION
LEE WRIGHT

Sports in the Time of Corona

Lee Wright is the RUF campus minister at the University of Texas at San Antonio (UTSA) and has recently transitioned from a six-year stint at the University of Central Florida. He is married to Sarah, an author and theologian. Lee holds a BS from Samford University and an MDiv and a MA in Counseling from Covenant Theological Seminary. Lee and Sarah have three children.

I've always been a fan. Some of my fondest memories are watching big games with friends and family. I witnessed three soccer games at the 1996 Olympics in Birmingham, Alabama. I was at an improbable comeback with a ninth-inning walkout home run in 2010. I went to the top of the sports mountain by going to the 2011 World Series with dear friends. Every Fourth of July my wife's family takes us to PNC Park to see the Pittsburgh Pirates. Sports has always been a huge part of my life.

As a child, if there were a place to check Sports as my religion, I would have done so. Everything in my life revolved around sports. I was athletically competitive. I was equally competitive as a fanboy.

Much changed in my life in college. The Good News of Jesus began taking root in my heart, and it made me realize the greater prize was found in Jesus not in the medals hanging in my room. I connected with the illustrations of an athlete exhibiting self-control (1 Cor. 9:25) and running the race (Heb. 12:2) because these aspects of my life were inhabiting my spiritual change.

The religion I have lost in quarantine is not my faith in Jesus. It's the religion that's been completely stripped of me, the one I had to fast from during quarantine—being a fan.

In his book *You Are What You Love*, author and philosopher James KA Smith writes that the heart can love something it doesn't intellectually believe. We can be drawn into love without knowing that it shapes our hearts. Smith uses the illustration of the shopping mall, and how its signage and mystique draw the consumer into an experience that transcends life itself.[1] I feel this as I walk through the entrances to a field or stadium. I even experience it in my living room through a television screen as the pre-game show, or the montage before a big game, draws me into the moment. It's as though I'm entering something that is special, other, maybe even holy.

As an avid fan I have felt the burden of no live sports since the coronavirus shutdown.

On March 9th and 10th, I attended back-to-back Spring Training day games in the lovely, sweaty central Florida sun. Spring Training is a wonderful experience. Spectators witness aspiring athletes compete to be on the prized Major League Baseball team roster. The Spring Training experience is so pure. Players do not have their names on the back of their jerseys, there is little fanfare around the game, and many players are striving for a place on the team. For some it's been years of work, and their families are longing to see them "make it." I long for the February day when pitchers and catchers report, because the game I love comes back. Spring Training signals the beginning of the liturgy of flourishing.

These pre-coronavirus games were different, though, and it felt like a wave was coming. On March 9th in lovely Bradenton, Florida, concession workers, ticket agents, and fellow spectators were taking a little more precaution than usual in the quaint LECOM Stadium. At this point, there was little concern that the MLB season, much less life as we knew it, would be delayed, though Manatee County where this game was being played, was the first place coronavirus had been confirmed in the state of Florida. In spite of the threat, this was Spring Training, and The Show Must Go On!

Then on March 10th, as more cases were found, there seemed to be no fear among patrons of the Yankees-Blue Jays game at George Steinbrenner Field in Tampa. The average age of the crowd being 70 years-old, I commented on an Instagram photo, "Great ballpark. Lots of elderly people unafraid of COVID-19" and I sat with 20,000 other people. We had no idea the world was about to turn upside down.

The evening of March 10th I read Yascha Mounk's article in The Atlantic titled *Cancel Everything* where the notion that social distancing was the only means to stop COVID-19 in its tracks.[2] It never dawned on me that my rhythm would be completely turned upside down. My liturgy would be halted.

The following day, the unthinkable happened. Utah Jazz star Rudy Gobert tested positive for coronavirus. Another teammate tested positive the following day. Then the entire NBA suspended all games.

I sat stunned on March 12th as college basketball shut down. Conference tournaments were cancelled. A day later March Madness was finished. And then Spring Training was closed. MLB Opening Day was suspended. The NBA and NHL seasons saw no hope for re-entry. The Masters was postponed. Everything was truly being cancelled.

I could go on about the shutdowns in sports, but I am sitting in my house during a time when the television is typically blowing up with sports and sports news, and the only live sports must be witnessed in the early hours in the morning— broadcasts of baseball from South Korea (and Slippery Stairs and weird near-belly-flop diving from Norway). At this point with three children at home, I had to completely fast from my love, and it wasn't even a Lenten choice.

Coronavirus took my love. But this love was offering me little in return.

The Lord has done some necessary heart work in this time. I have begun to see my very real over-attachment to sports, and that could only be found in a complete shutdown. Spring particularly hits me, and my competitive heart feels satisfied in something that it loves far too much. I feel more alive because of the anticipation and quality of exciting sports. My spirit is lifted, and then there's something else right around the corner!

In 1993, Connie Chung interviewed Michael Jordan. She asked him if he has a true gambling problem. Jordan's answer was, "I don't have a gambling problem. I can stop at any time. I have a competitive problem. A competition problem."[3]

I could choose to not go to Spring Training one season, but I'll need to fill my sports fix some other way. I found it one summer in watching competitive corn hole. When we moved to Orlando, I followed the Orlando City Soccer Club. The excitement around the city was electric. The marketing was top-notch. And there was pride in wearing the purple kit or donning an Orlando City hat. I love being a fan because it draws me in to a story. For the Orlando City narrative, it drew me and my family into the city we lived in and helped us signal to our neighbors that we belonged.

The fasting from sports was so good for me because I saw my religious fervor for sports. I believe that my heart will be satisfied in competitiveness, even if it comes at a loss. The longing for competition centers my satisfaction in my own performance or that of my team's.

During the coronavirus Holy Week, I was awestruck by the goodness Jesus displayed during the week between Palm Sunday and Resurrection Day. On the cross Jesus says, "It is finished" in the way we long for after a long season cheering for the team to climb the highest mountain. But the best news, something we cannot compete with in sports, is the resurrection, where Jesus' victory was announced when the angel said, "The tomb is empty."

The competitive heart needs such good words. It has been finished, and you didn't do anything to accomplish it. Jesus did it all. Jesus won. We can rejoice once and for all. We can cling to the one true story that has been accomplished for us all.

I'm not sure what my sports longings will look like once life is back to normal, but I believe my rhythm has been thrown off so much that I no longer look toward the kingdom of the World Series, or NBA Finals, or the awarding of a green jacket for my satisfaction and fervor. On my street I watch kids playing games together and dads playing HORSE with their sons. I can't wait to coach my kids. My daughter loves going to our back yard to swing her junior golf clubs. I am eager to see them grasp baseball and understand what's happening in a game.

Sports will continue to have a special place in my heart, but it is not ultimate. Jesus came to conquer the longings of our hearts and take us from death to life. He died so that we might live and awake to the loves that overtake our heart.

I need to fast more. I need to fast from things that give me satisfaction. I need to find my true religion in Jesus and reject false religions. My heart is still prone to find ultimate satisfaction in sports, but God is faithful, and I must remember his goodness in my life.

---

1. James KA Smith, *You Are What You Love: The Spiritual Power of Habit.* (Grand Rapids, MI: Brazos Press, 2016), 46ff.

2. Yascha Mounk, *The Atlantic*, March 10, online edition. https://www. theatlantic.com/ideas/archive/2020/03/coronavirus-cancel-everything/607675/.

3. July 15, 1993 "Eye to Eye with Connie Chung." This segment re-aired on the documentary The Last Dance, ESPN and Netflix, on May 3, 2020.

IN SICKNESS AND IN HEATH, TIL DEATH DO US PART

DOUG SERVEN

Weddings in the Time of Corona

————

*Doug is Senior Pastor at City Pres in Oklahoma City. He has jour-
nalism degrees from the University of Missouri-Columbia (BJ) and
the University of Oklahoma (MPW). He graduated from
Covenant Theological Seminary (MDiv). After his ordination in
the Presbyterian Church in America (PCA), Doug served for ten
years as the Reformed University Fellowship (RUF) campus
minister in Norman, Oklahoma, before beginning City Pres. He is
married to Julie, and they have four children.*

————

"Let's do it this Friday."

That's what a fianceé might say when she realizes all
her wedding plans have been obliterated because of the
coronavirus. We might be talking through the various
options: they postpone until the fall, or her fiancé moves
in with her because he won't have a place to live, or what
happens when shelter in place is over? However, when we
get to the This Friday Plan, I say, "Good decision!"

I love weddings. I've performed over sixty of them,

and they're all great. I don't usually go to the biggest over-the-top or destination weddings (I don't know that many wealthy people I suppose), but I've been to some show stoppers. Beautiful venues, amazing bands, full bars, seven-course meals. Those blow-out parties are memorable.

But I also love the small ones. You don't have to spend tens of thousands of dollars to get married.

One couple got married between church services. He'd been released from jail, and they didn't want to wait. I married a homeless couple we'd befriended at church. Another couple had been living together for years and years, but after a few months of coming to church, they decided they didn't want to keep doing that anymore. We married them that week. One couple didn't want to go through a big wedding (she'd been married before), and they invited friends for a cocktail hour before the wedding, and then they did it afterwards. For another couple, the groom's orders from the military were changed. He was told he had to report to Alaska six months before he was supposed to. The bride wouldn't have been able to move and live with him unless they were married. We were friends from the gym, so I was the only pastor she knew. She called me on Sunday, and they were married on Wednesday.

We've have a rather cosmic reason for this quick, small wedding now. While those other ones were personal decisions for personal reasons, we have had a world-wide, big pandemic on our hands. I've been encouraging couples to go ahead and do it. Now's the time. Throw a party later when you have time to think about it.

Because—while weddings are cool parties often times (though that's not necessary)—it's all about the marriage. The wedding will pass. It's one day. It's really a few hours or minutes. It can be stressful and bittersweet. It's a strange day for the participants, and tempers can flare. Everything seems like it can be ruined by a mom, or a snide remark, or a late groomsman, or a sassy bridesmaid.

You've pored over that invite list, and only half of the people RSVPed. The cake is lopsided. The photographer didn't capture the ambiance.

The marriage is the thing. When you know you're in love, and you've found the one you want to vow to, you want to do it as soon as possible. The virus is an opportunity to move things up and get things done.

A man and a woman make a covenantal vow to be together for as long as they both shall live, in sickness and in health, til death do they part:

> I, take you, to be my wedded husband/wife. And I do promise before God and these witnesses that I will be true to you, forsaking all others, keeping myself only for you from this day forward, to have and to hold, to love and to cherish, to honor and respect in the midst of all God brings to us, so long as we both shall live.

That's a picture for us of the love of Christ for the church (though not the only picture by any means). We have a feast coming up at the marriage supper of the lamb, which we read about in Revelation:

> *Then I heard what seemed to be the voice of a great multitude, like the roar of many waters and like the sound of mighty peals of thunder, crying out,*
> *"Hallelujah! For the Lord our God the Almighty reigns.*
> *Let us rejoice and exult and give him the glory,*
> *for the marriage of the Lamb has come, and his Bride has made herself ready;*
> *it was granted her to clothe herself with fine linen, bright and pure"—*
>
> *for the fine linen is the righteous deeds of the saints.*
> *And the angel said to me, "Write this: Blessed are those who are invited to the marriage supper of the Lamb." And he said to me, "These are the true words of God." (Rev. 19:6–9)*

The marriage is the thing. The wedding gets you there. We will feast together at a wedding reception soon enough.

A wedding only needs five people—the bride and groom, the officiant, and two witnesses. Everything else is extra. You still might want to take a photo or two (or just put it all on Facebook live), but you've made the photographer's job a lot easier. You might buy the (Presbyterian) minister a nice scotch, but he's most likely relieved he doesn't have to sit and make small talk with your uncle during the reception.

Times of stress can force decisions. Be careful not to marry the wrong person in the midst of this lonely time. I'll still ask if you wholeheartedly, without reservation, wish to do this, and that you're not being forced or pressured by anyone, even by yourself. You are free to wait to make it 100 percent sure.

When you're ready, now's the time. We can expect much more partying in the new heavens and the new earth.

AFTERWORD

In the title of Márquez' novel, *El Amor in Los Tiempos del Cólera*, the word *cólera* has a double meaning. It's translated as Cholera—the bacterial disease that ravaged Colombia—but it also means anger, ire, or passion. Márquez intended for his readers to imagine a time of both widespread death and emotional unrest.

Corona, too, is a Spanish play on words. It refers to the coronavirus SARS-CoV-2, of course, but in Spanish, corona simply means crown.

Our coronavirus has made a claim of authority upon our world. In doing so, he has shown himself to be a brutal and malevolent dictator. His kingdom is universal and his reign has ushered in a regime of disruption in every nation and sphere of life.

Yet the kingdom of SARS-CoV-2, like all earthly crowns, will come to an end. There is only room in this cosmos for one king, and he has many names: Immanuel, Prince of Peace, Wonderful Counselor, Ancient of Days, Jesus the Christ.

King Jesus reigns even now. He reigns over nations and leaders, families and workplaces, in universities halls and cafes. He even reigns over margaritas and smoked brisket; over tears of lament and sad goodbyes.

Hopefully, the stories of this book serve as a testimony

to the universal kingdom of Christ. There are of course more stories to be told. If all the stories of faith, hope, and love in the time of Corona were told, all the libraries in the world couldn't hold them. Perhaps someday we will get to hear them all and see them through the lens of redemption.

There will come a day when SARS-CoV-2 is put under the foot of Christ and crushed like he deserves. On that day, all those who put their faith in the crucified messiah will reign triumphant over everything that has cursed humanity and the universe. St. Paul even tells us that we, too, will get to participate in the crushing (Rom. 16:20)!

Can you imagine that day? Can you imagine the day when your foot gets to crush sin, death, and the devil? Can you imagine the day when you stand upon the neck of SARS-CoV-2 and cancers of all kinds, divorce and domestic abuse, rape and murder, oppression and injustice, futility and despair, headaches and scraped knees, envy and strife, lust and slander, everything sad and ugly and inhumane? Can you imagine lifting your resurrected foot with Christ and the saints and bidding goodbye to the sin and sorrow of this world?

No more death. No more sin. No one to curse humanity. Only life and peace and joy everlasting.

What a day that will be. It will be a day for feasting, and feast we will. Lord, hasten the day! Come Lord Jesus. Come quickly. Amen.

A LITANY FOR COVID-19

O God the Father, Creator of heaven and earth and
all human bodies,
Have mercy upon us.
O God the Son, who took on flesh to redeem the
world,
Have mercy upon us.
O God the Holy Spirit, Comforter and Counselor,
Have mercy upon us.
O holy, blessed, and glorious Trinity, one God,
Have mercy upon us.

For those who cough,
For those who have a fever,
For those who suffer from COVID-19 now and in
the coming weeks,
Lord, have mercy.

For those who feel anxiety over their symptoms,
For those who fear death and disease,
For all who are scared,
Lord, have mercy.

For those with chronic pain,
For those who are ill,

For all who suffer the ailments of the human body,
Lord, have mercy.

For the doctors who treat the ill,
For the nurses who care for the dying,
For the support staff that make hospitals run,
Lord, have mercy.

For the child stuck at home,
For the mother and father who nurture children,
For the siblings who struggle to love,
Lord, have mercy.

For the unborn babies,
For the pregnant mothers,
For the celibate and barren,
Lord, have mercy.

For the marriages in strife,
For those who live alone,
For those homebound in unsafe homes,
Lord, have mercy.

For the retired and empty nesters,
For the widows and widowers,
For the elderly living in shared communities and
those who serve them,
Lord, have mercy.

For the leaders of nations,
For the governors of states,
For the mayors of cities and all who lead others,
Lord, have mercy.

For those working from home,
For the online learner,
For the technologically isolated,
Lord, have mercy.

For the furloughed workers,
For the unemployed and uninsured,
For all those living with reduced income,
Lord, have mercy.

For the orphans and children in foster care,
For those living without homes,
For the refugee and the immigrant,
Lord, have mercy.

For the chefs and line cooks,
For the bartenders and baristas,
For all who prepare meals for the hungry and show
hospitality,
Lord, have mercy.

For those who weep without ending,
For those who struggle to control their anger,
For those who find it hard to wait,
Lord, have mercy.

In our failures to love you and our neighbor,
In the idols our hearts depend on for security,
In all our vices, habits, and addictions that emerge
in stressful times,
Lord, have mercy.

For the pastors, elders, and deacons seeking to care
for their flocks,
For the youth and children's ministry directors
who nurture young souls,
For worship directors who lead us in praise and
lament,
Lord, have mercy.

For your church in the world,
For all who work to support her,
For all who depend on her for nurture,

Lord, have mercy.

For every person made by your hand,
For every human who bears your image,
For all people in every place,
Lord, have mercy.

ACKNOWLEDGMENTS

I would like to thank every author who contributed their stories and thoughts to this book—much hard work and honesty went into these pages. Thanks especially to Doug Serven and the folks at White Blackbird Books for the opportunity to make this available to a wider audience. Many thanks also to Jason Bueno for his creative work in designing the cover of the book. Lastly, I'd like to thank my wife Katie and my children—Jasper, Nina, and Felix— for bearing the image of Christ to me daily in the time of Corona. It's been hard, but you make it worth it.

—Joshua Burdette, General Editor